D1784181

Aya Samuel
People Power
Protest

All rights reserved. No part of this book may be reprinted, reproduced in any form or by any means, electronic, digital or mechanical means including information storage or retrieval now or any future invention without the written permission of the author or publisher.

Copyright © 2024 Aya Samuel

Aya Samuel has asserted rights as the author under the Patents and Copyright Act 1988.

A revised edition

Paper used is FSC certified through the Climate
Friendly Pledge

Cover images taken from the various protest, remembrance by Aya Samuel

BPUK Review by Book Printing UK

A Self Published Book

Apologise for any errors or omissions

Dedicated to all those who fought for freedom and fight for justice

CONTENTS

Preface   9

Introduction: Freedom and Justice   11

Apartheid in the East   27

Stopped Searched Shot or Killed   37

BLM Protest Brutality   43

Stand Up To Racism   89

Covid Uncovered   105

Reparations March   109

United Families & Friends Campaign   129

Windrush Betrayal   145

Remembering Grenfell   151

Commonwealth War Memorial   159

Mandela   163

Patrisse and Angela at WOW   167

Black Lives Matter   171

Grenfell One Year On   179

Grenfell Remembrance Walls   191

References   229

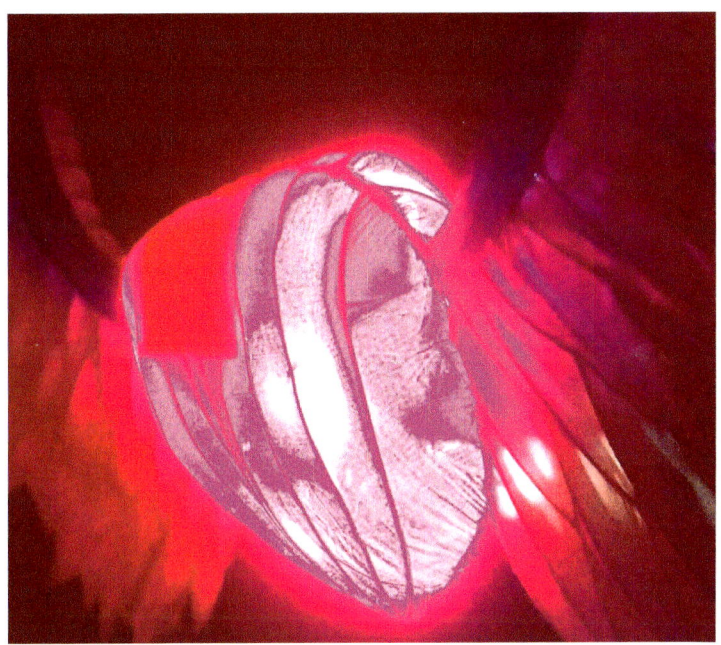

"Our beating heart is shaking the wings of friends in high places, Angels." Aya Samuel

PREFACE

This book is primarily about the need for a new kind of education which is the 3 Rs Reckoning, Reparations and Redeeming and permission, position and privilege to explore black or ethnic history. It started as a much larger project of mine over eight years ago culminating in being part of a major protest as an activist. Although I grew up in a diverse area of London from a multicultural background, as a youngster at school I faced direct verbal racism on one occasion being called a "black bastard". Big mistake! A fight ensued and this was the last time I would hear these words directed at me. Covert forms such as "black board", "black coffee", and "white socks in black shoes", left me questioning. I delved into social studies as a young person but the focus was more on class and less about race and racism.

There was some reporting of the actual struggles on the streets, but this was often turned into a "riot" instead of what is fuelling the difficulties that black people face in Britain or the US. I came to understand that black history is serving as a challenger toward a legacy of oppression and all that stems from it, racial discrimination and inequalities. However, I realised that these particular concerns are very specific and had to be addressed on their own for a people with unique experiences and a history within the structural, sustaining, system of feudal mutation. This book is in its raw uncooked state to keep it as authentic as possible. The stories are mainly told in colour images while the words act as an anchor in the process of storytelling; in a narrative where the people are the stories within these pages as they become a *living* memorial. On the front cover, the first image shows two pieces of canvases transformed into powerful messages, holding symbolism. This is in the earliest language of childlike innocence, handprints. The third image emphasising state violence yet, "The splattering, spillage of innocent blood must not be in vain." It shall not be in vain for they were from a wonderful and no one can ever take that away even if they tried.

INTRODUCTION: FREEDOM AND JUSTICE

There are many other conflicts in the world that deserve more coverage and protest because of the length of time the struggles have been going on and the sheer scale of the conflict such as in Africa's Sudan. Low media coverage effacing the reality of the sufferings where according to Human Rights Watch, *7 million* people have been displaced and yet no outcry. Why? I have chosen to focus on Gaza first because the majority of those suffering are children and mothers or women from targeted Israeli airstrikes in just over three months and how this indignation, sparked, motivated, mobilised and organised a collective conscious response in the form of protest in many parts of the world. One of the biggest protests in London took place on 11 November 2023 to witness over 700,000 protesters take to the streets in solidarity with Palestinians facing displacement.

Our human rights are being breached and it is eroding as I write this page because there is another war, a war on people of colour, which has been going on for hundreds of years and continues its legacy due to structural, systemic, racism and brutality. The parallels between Black people and Palestinians are quite profound in terms of brutality, trauma, raids, execution, incarceration, racial discrimination, inequalities and deprivation. In the US police officers are sent to Israel to be live-trained by the military especially on how to disperse protesters using violence and the use of surveillance technologies a pack that binds them together. This kind of mentality has already seeped into European countries such as Britain and France. On 27 June 2023, in Nanterre Paris, Nahel Merzouk a 17-year-old boy of Algerian and Moroccan heritage was shot dead at point-blank range by armed French police. On 7 January 2023, 29-year-old Tyre Nichols a young black man and father was traffic stopped by five police officers in Memphis, Tennessee which led to his death three days later. On 5 September 2022, Chris Kaba an unarmed young black man was shot dead by armed police in South

London. In the US it took just over three weeks for a guilty verdict on all three counts to be given by the jury in this *historic* trial in the killing of George Floyd, on 25 May 2020, in Minnesota, Wisconsin. The maximum sentence was up to 40 years but this person who shall remain nameless in this book only got 22.5 years much less than was expected for this crime.[1] Black Lives Matter, BLM, is a theme that stretches far back centuries at least thousands of years ago and black history is all year round. In more recent years, months, weeks and days BLM has become extremely prominent mentioned 30 million times on social media alone in 2020 in a war of police brutality, racial hatred and discrimination inflicted.[2] To fight these injustices we must know our ancient history as the earliest civilisation as rulers and what we are fighting for because this is not new. Their system just keeps mutating because they haven't stopped to hear I mean *listen* since Africa began to be stolen and subsequently, divided.

The Phoenicians, Assyrians, Persians, Greeks, Romans, Arabs and Europeans all had their share of taking land and gaining control over Egypt. It was known as Kemet in Africa my ancestral country using the knowledge from Egypt and particularly plundering the gold coast which was perceived as lucrative because of its gold which was converted into wealth. I am part of a Diaspora because in terms of European involvement from around the sixteenth century onwards over 22 million African people were stolen and forced into an enslaved migration system.[3] Africans including women and children were trafficked in chains to the coast, fortresses, then onto the Beast across the Atlantic and if they survived auctioned off or resold in what became known as the *Triangular* Trade. This created huge wealth, 'A substantial boost to the growth of Liverpool, Bristol and London.'[4] But, this traumatic processing of people freights a crime against our humanity, was just the beginning of breaking into plantation life. Based on a hostile environment of forced labour, deprivation, cruelty and abuse against a lavish lifestyle from the produce of particularly Jamaican gang sugar 11 million tons of it. Not to mention the cotton, rice and tobacco trade.[5] Yet, beyond courage our freedom fighters such as Queen Nzingha fought to keep Ndonga, modern Angola, from Portuguese control in the 1600s; the Maroons, Ashanti tribes, in the 1730s fought the British army as a free people until around the 1790s. But, this "harvested" of black bodies produced forty per cent of cotton by 1.8 million black Americans.[6] This prized cotton spinning into cloth in the north of England.

Moreover, even though no legislation existed in England to support slavery, runaways were hunted or sold including children shown in a new Glasgow database. This highlights the heroic role of runaways in the struggle for freedom despite a landmark ruling for James Somerset in 1772. Quobna Cuguano wrote to newspapers and the monarchy about the, 'Wickedness of slavery' in his book in 1787. He was only 13 when having survived the fortress and Beast of the Middle Passage enduring, the clattering of shackles and slapping of whips he was sold in Grenada onto a sugar plantation a legacy linked with my family to this day. Brought to England in 1772 he was able to gain his freedom but remembered those who were still enslaved even as house slaves because they still, were not free.

This made him a powerful force as an Abolitionist and campaigner the first to openly state the moral right and duty to defy the *entire* slave trade and fight against it, "That they should carry on traffic of the most barbarous cruelty and injustice."[7] To stop anyone from eating the sugar they were hit across the face to knock the teeth out of their mouth. This was the extent of their cruel, brutal and absolute inhumanity of forced separation and breaking into plantation living. Olaudah Equiano, a prince from the Igbo tribe, was abducted as a child and torn from his sister but became an Abolitionist, Sons of Africa, through his own very personal experiences, intense campaigning, and petitioning the UK government in 1791. His best seller was published in 1789, where he writes about wishing for death as a companion and when he wouldn't eat, someone would grip his hands tightly holding him fast onto a winch while another thrashed his back relentlessly.[8] Thus, turning public opinion which eventually leads to the ending of the *transatlantic* crossings by Britain although other countries continued this oppression. Toussaint's army fought the French for St. Domingue's, Ayiti's freedom declared in 1804.[9] While Yaa Asantewaa fought the British army in 1900 for the liberation of Ghana.[10] Independence was finally gained in the 1950s by Kwame Nkrumah who became President of Ghana.

Others such as Nat Turner in *The Birth of a Nation* devised an Uprising.[11] Sam Sharpe in Jamaica leads the Christmas Day Revolt in 1831 on the Kensington Estate. Harriet Tubman, the female hero, took huge risks to free her family and hundreds more fittingly called, "Moses" and vividly portrayed in the film *Harriet*.[12] She also suffered from poor health and injury to her head. But, the threat of being sold was so great a Charlestown advert of May 7, 1835 reads, 'Highest price for Men, Women & Children' as families were torn apart in one auction forcibly split up never to be seen again.[13] I am trying to imagine this unimaginable reality to have my family standing on a platform, on display, for the highest bidder ready to be sold to some merciless enslaver.

Another advert shows the, 'Great Sale of Slaves' in Lewis County 1855, which included a young woman with a 6-month-old baby and 17 children from 12 years upwards.[14] The depth of this inhumanity of slavery is indescribable. In addition, fugitive and slave codes were established as early as 1661 by the British to deter running away.[15] These codes were then enacted into Law in Virginia in 1705 and across the colonies.[16] These included being branded with a hot iron as property exposed in the documentary *A 1000 Years A Slave* exposing the impact of slavery as well as heritage with many well-known persons such as Sir Trevor Mcdonald whose words are so poignant about the way that slavery was designed to treat black people as less than human.[17] Whippings or punishments were at the will of the enslaver, there would be no weapons, arms, reading or writing and *permission* to marry was some of the codes. An 1850's poster against these codes says that it, 'Disregards all the ordinary securities of personal liberty.'[18] On the run, you are a fugitive.[19] But, the many uprisings throughout the Caribbean Bussa in Barbados[20] Fedon in 1795 Grenada[21] and Chief Tacky in 1760 Jamaica put pressure on the dynamics of the politics of the Abolition movement as many of rebellions in the British West Indian territories contributed enormously to the movement for abolition.[22]

So great was the fear of revolt, even at sea, as in Amistad in 1839. The leader of the revolt was Joseph Cinqué on this ship carrying 53 other captives, including girls. The experiences lead to a landmark court case in the US when in 1840 some captives gained their freedom, from those who survived.[23] The film *Emperor* tells the true story of Sheilds Green who in 1858 at great cost escaped plantation life.[24] His journey led him to Frederick Douglass a wonderful orator, "With just such pathos and outrage Douglass evoked the sufferings" of his people. He came to Britain and joined other Abolitionists who took huge risks for freedom, rights and equality. His newspaper was called the North Star, which he edited in New York.[25]

Others such as Sarah Remond came to Britain and also influenced the Abolition movement as an Abolitionist. Her brother Charles Remond also came to Britain for the first World Anti-Slavery Convention in London addressing crowds. He became famous for his speeches and was also part of the Underground Railroad and would have known Harriet the "Conductor" during this crucial time which made such a difference to the families that escaped, hoping, for a better life. This struggle was also articulated by so many such as Mary Prince, who was born in the Bahamas in 1788, and was only 12 when she was separated and sold for £38. She was often beaten or flogged and worked for long hours in the salt field packaging. She was very remarkable because she was the first black woman to petition the government on Anti-Slavery. Her autobiography of 1831 contains, 'The horrors of slavery.'[26] How the notion of it ached her being. Despite this slavery mutated into colonial rule while our country was *looted* and raided by the British army. They auctioned these off as collections or art a mutation of selling African people, many of which are in museums in Germany or the US.[27]

However, the race for Africa and the subsequent dividing meant that the Transatlantic Abolition Bill of 1807 and 1838 did not end the oppression of African descendants over two hundred years ago as Europeans invaded and began a colonial conquest of the African land in the 1800s. From the 1890s, the German occupation of Namibia led to what is called the *Black Holocaust* from the1890s up to the 1940s in camps of torture and medical experiments.[28] Here again, effacing our history so that we do not remember and the truth is obscured yet it is now a time of revealing the truth. So, there is a double Black Holocaust and now modern, mutated, methods of systematic violation, racism, discrimination, profiling and targeting of especially young black boys and adult males as well as our women.

This is on a scale that draws attention from the United Nations meaning that 2015-2024 became the International Decade for People of African Descent. The former Secretary-General of the UN Ban Ki-Moon said, "People of African descendant are among those most affected by racism."[29] They confront abuse of their human rights. Even as I write this passage the mass protest carried on for many weeks across the US from Minnesota to New York to California to Atlanta to Washington. Beyond a moment in time but rather something that mushroomed reaching into ours and future generations. In the meantime, we have a struggle on our hands the struggle for our "Fee'dom." I used the word, Fee'dom here to symbolise our fight as this was spoken by a very young child when asked, "What do you want?"[30] Back on 2-7 May 1963 over 1,000 children walked out of their classrooms and marched against a system that denied them their basic rights. It was called the Children's Crusade because they knew then that, education is not just in their classrooms but risking their own lives against a brutal system, very much in existence, continuing to fight for justice. Similarly, the BLM, Black Lives Matter, movement was born in 2013 as a response to the outright brutality and injustices toward black people. In the killing of Trayvon Martin on 26 February 2012 a minor, with no one held accountable. The co-founder of BLM Patrisse Khan-Cullors spoke at the WOW, Women of the World, festival on 9 March 2018, "No More" and about what led to the movement's beginning.[31] Quite fittingly, BLM has been nominated for the Noble Peace Prize.

Angela Davis also graced us with her presence at the WOW festival on 8 March 2019 just hearing her speak I realised how easily it could have been very different if not for her sheer determination despite being pursued by the feds. Similarly, like other Panthers who were also incarcerated or shot. Walter Rodney, a black activist was killed for his speaking out and writing about Europe's underdevelopment of Africa which is still very relevant today. Malcolm X declared in Paris, on 23 November 1964: "The only reason that the present generations of white Americans are in a position of economic strength...is because their fathers worked our fathers for over 400 years with no pay."[32] Black people are continually being used or exploited commercially to big up brands a mutation of branding or too big up Britain; doing us a disservice especially straight after Black History Month, Cashing our Culture. Why not call it White Friday or any other colour? We must peel back the layers because of the implications for black people economically. He was very forceful about African identity from his childhood traumas such as the destruction of his home, lynching and losing both his parents at a tender age which influenced his life and outlook.[33] He is now celebrated on Malcolm X Day, 19 May 1925, for his fearlessness and being proud of his heritage. He was also about unity and how as a people this would make them stronger more empowered to confront a system that mistreats them, despite their solidarity. This is why this time is a time of reckoning, reparations and redeeming a time to settle the Accounts in terms of the Great Debt for *unpaid* labour and the loss of bloodlines, lineages, African names, languages, cultural traditions, ancestral customs and land rights. As well as inheriting not wealth, but the current inequalities that black people face exposed even more by the ravaging of covid and the rising cost of living due to inflation for food, fuel, rents and the control of debt.[34] The Windrush betrayal is another example. The destruction of Grenfell is a betrayal because no one has been brought to Justice and the inquiry is still ongoing, prolonged, with no accountability upheld.

The documentary about 100,000 unnamed African and "forgotten" soldiers during World War One were not given the heroic honour they deserved striking at the core. Forgetting is not the same as choosing not to remember in other words it is more about concealment.[35] The French government gave the Statue of Liberty to America in the 1876 centenary of independence despite the fact that millions of African people were still enslaved in America during the French Revolution. Yet, twelve presidents were enslavers and the US constitution claimed that all men, no women, were created equal I note not *born* equal because of slavery. The first president I shall only give initials was sworn into office as an enslaver, G.W. The enslaved were worked like a ship "below deck" in the basement areas. He had a very large house but only a small two-roomed space next to a washroom and smokehouse for them.[36] Even worse, only five feet from what is known as the Liberty Bell Centre which was being repositioned as part of a project. This would have erased the room area had it not been for protest and campaigning to get to the truth of the Africans who lived in this house. One of them was a brave woman named Ona Maria

Judge, who managed to escape to freedom around 1797. When she was interviewed in 1845 she said, "I should never get my liberty."[37] In Virginia despite the fact that the Womb Act of 1784, conferred freedom to her child. However, through the constitutional rights of liberty Ona applied it directly to herself to win freedom. Clearly, this constitution must be amended to include native and black Americans and others who were earlier groups of people long before modern America. Haitians also fought for their independence but were impoverished by the French who demanded a huge payout in exchange for independence.

However, in 2019 while I was on the train, I heard a lady speaking very loudly in French to lots of children. I thought it was rather rare but on Monday 15 April 2019 a fire started around 5.43 am in the famous Notre Dame Cathedral in France.

By Tuesday morning the steeple had gone and over *400* fire-fighters were dealing with the emergency. It was such a sight because the history of the building is over 850-year-old in the heart of the city.[38] The strange thing is that the huge cross at the pulpit was illuminated and the same shape formed on the building. What is the connection here? Buildings can be rebuilt but it is our history that needs repairing or *Redeeming* over 400 years; not a building from the old paradigm which is not part of the new era consciousness of awakening at this time. This is why Reparations Justice is so crucial in our time and the Annual March takes place from Brixton, Windrush Square, London, near the Black Cultural Archives. This is on 1 August, 1 Mosiah, after Marcus Garvey the first major Pan-African and social entrepreneur of the Black Star Liner which is now a monument in Accra, Ghana. In 1914, he founded the UNIA, Universal Negro Improvement Association, and in 1920 New York he led the first convention, Garvey was a crusader for people of African heritage to take pride and bear the torch of freeing Africa from Europe.[39] He also produced black dolls instead of the caucasian ones that flooded the market an example of what I call, economic whitening where the market is the arena for conditioning certain ideas or values of whiteness. He had millions of followers and came to London in 1912, working on his magazine called *African Times*. I would suggest that World War I and II were ways to weaken what he was achieving to strengthen Africa's economy and resources as these wars relied heavily on Africa to gain what was perceived as a victory in Europe at that time. This also brings to my mind the fact that although Christianity began in Judah it was "converted" into a Westernised institution and this was used and continues to be used to whitewash and subjugate our people.

There is a need for awareness of this process so that we can unlearn the kind of concepts or conditioning that we are being taught to begin a different identity consciousness. For example, the prevailing image that Adam and Eve were white instead of what became known as African, even in Africa.

When it is as clear as daylight that Africa is a Black continent where the earliest people came from and lived and migrated long before anyone else.[40] Clearly, this truth has been whitewashed which means that the first man being black African was directly made by God who, 'Breathed into his nostrils the breath of life.'[41] Then the male became a living person. Therein, lays the crux of the matter. Do you see the connection with, "I Can't Breathe?" Moreover, the language and culture of the oppressor speaks of a homogeneous world and what I call the stripping of our colour. Yet, black African people come from the earliest civilisation, this means that humanity was birthed by Africans, a historical fact.[42] This is the *cradle* of humanity. Africa's Great Civilisations as kings, queens, princes, princesses and warriors are not defined by colour. But, by tribes and our Jewish ancestry Ashanti, Igbo, Benin, Nubians, Kush, Mandinka, Yoruba, Bantu and Lemba. Beating Drums. Yes, "They couldn't take our beating hearts from us then or now". We *are* the drums that keep on beating![43] Moreover, I am claiming my ancestral African presence in

England since ancient times and through the Nubians who traded with the Greeks and Minoans who travelled to Britain over 4,000 years ago B.C.[44] They came from France to the coast of Britain long before the Romans. But, where is our memorial to those who came before us? I am putting the colour of black back into storytelling this black history where it rightly and truly belongs and in doing so black people become a *living* memorial. However, we are still living with legacies of even more now with huge wealth hoarded by virus-like, massive, mutated, multinational plantation owners in their legacy of complete exploitation. Especially, in the absolute saturation of chocolate, the new gold, the second biggest where 45 per cent of it comes from Ghana, the West coast of Africa. Plus, coffee, tea, and tobacco industries with the so-called "fair-trade" logo marketing ploy; it is all about the supply chains and non ethical values.

For a very long time now there have been campaigns to bring ethical accountability to major companies. Even more shocking, is the fact that thousands of *child* labourers are being trafficked to farms by, 'Employing children they were expected to work in hazardous conditions' and perform damaging tasks.[45] This is by those sacrificing Child Human Rights. Over £60 billion is made from the Ivory Coast yet a day's wage is only a meagre $0.50. However, in Washington D.C a lawsuit has been filed against the major chocolate companies such as Cadburys, Quakers since the 1890s, Hershey, Nestle and Mars who have thousands of children in their supply chains causing them harm. They continue to make massive profits from their exploitations allowing them to cream off the wealth.[46] This modern mutated form of capitalism enables them the funds to reconfigure the city. This goes for the clothing, fashion and toy industries effacing the reality of the production process especially through advertising. We need to know the whole process beforehand to make the right ethical choices. Gandhi and Martin Luther King Jr., wished for a World of peace and the late Mandela made Peace his greatest weapon through his life and sacrifices. He founded what is called, "The Elders" world leaders with a passion for equality.[47] Young adults are part of this too with many dynamic groups and organisations already having such an impact as Global Citizens. Furthermore, the atrocities against our people are pushing the movement forward even more. From what I have observed mainly younger people took a stand in the US in 2020 despite being faced with the military and riot police on the opposite side. I think that it must have taken a great deal of courage to defy these curfews and take a stand to be counted in the crowd. Still, even then, there is an expansion of mass incarceration due to a budget of over 40 per cent for, "Social workers with guns."[48] As told by Professor Khalil Muhammad instead of service and protection. Often, I have observed that rights are not read and reasons are not given when arrests are made in black communities. Even in drama, the weapon becomes normalised as the authority rather than protocol for the defenceless.

The Race Act of 1968 did not protect black people and around the same time, the story of the *Mangrove* community restaurant owned by Frank Crichlow was a prominent symbol of resistance. Shaun Parkes was nominated for 15 Baftas for his powerful performance as Frank Crichlow. Raids, a mutation of raiding Africa, harassment and intimidation by police in Notting Hill, London, become regular occurrences and a symbol of courage, defiance and justice during the 1960s. In the dramatised version the testimonies especially the final statement by Darcus Howe, who defended himself as a lawyer, captivated the jury, making history. As a Black Panther he fiercely spoke out about the power to defend not just himself but the power of the people or community to take a stand together against injustice.[49] In the Mangrove drama I really saw this defending in protest and the courts in a powerful way. This was a dynamic time of black struggle including the Oval 4 miscarriage of justice incarceration for over 40 years and the Stockwell 6, thereby, inspiring a new generation in the struggle.[50] This struggle is the same campaigning by United Family & Friends Campaign, UFFC, group to bring about justice and the challenges they face over 20 years since 1998. Fighting for transparency and justice for their loved ones who died in state custody and challenging the structural racism with the support of the charity, Inquest. The increased use of digital, android, facial, voice and fingerprinting AI technologies what I call, "Frankinsteining" by giving life to the machines, bypassing our consent with the use of algorithms. The extraction of personal data is called "surveillance capitalism" by Social Psychologist, Professor Shoshana Zuboff and how it can be used to *predict* behaviour through sinister motives.[51] I am thinking now about a kind of android diplomatic immunity and whether the companies owning or operating these digital technologies or AI may get to have this. The very fact that robots online are asking a human to confirm, "You are not a robot?"

When the lockdown happened on 23 March 2020 to stay at home with millions of texts sent out same day eerie and strange seeing the streets practically empty, human hibernating. But, seriously the Corona Virus Act 2020 reared its ugly head and has already deprived rights in the ban culture.[52] Yet, mass testing, vaccinations and hospital care as never before in the UK and much of the world costing millions was astounding in the crisis. In contrast, the regeneration sweeping across London and other cities is based on principles of ancient Kemet knowledge. This African knowledge is along the lines of the *Golden* Triangle sacred geometry or pi, the golden mean.[53] It was used during the renaissance or rebirth and now it is being utilised again to recreate £30 billion London as a new city primarily for a new type of clientele. This new professional lifestyle class a mutated form of plantation lifestyle intensifies while the real communities are mostly being priced out of the urban city. Effectively, this is taking the heart out of the community; I lived in North London many moons ago and now where I lived stands properties worth nearly half a million pounds! You only have to look at areas such as South, West, East London, Wembley and Hoxton areas that were once stigmatised now it is "cool" to live here with these exclusive homes and facilities creating new privatised spaces but not so family-friendly.[54] In terms of the regeneration that is going on, I would suggest that this regeneration gentrification is an attempt to erase black and ethnic history. For example, the Museum of London in East London fortified its columns to house the tons and tons of sugar from Jamaica in what I call the long stretch now part of the Docklands regeneration project from the 1980s. This was a huge trading complex in the luxury of conveniently forgetting 400 years of enslavement. The current site of Canary Wharf is the former West Indian Docks once a very busy slavery port, 'The World's largest docks...crucial' to London's economy.[55] But, thankfully, the Nubian Jak Community Trust is making sure of black heritage and history by establishing Blue Plaques on buildings or homes. On 17 May 2024 a plaque in honour of James Baldwin a civil rights activist was placed at Dalston Square, London where he visited in July 1985 during a national anti-racist campaign year.[56] More so, the Nubians were the earliest civilisation in the world, rulers or Pharaohs, in Ta-Seti Southern Egypt before the northern areas were developed.[57]

Another extraordinary story is about a black couple Ellen and William Craft who used disguise to escape slavery. They managed to get to Britain becoming part of the Abolition movement; Julian-Ellen Craft great-great granddaughter said why they risked so much because, they didn't want their offspring to be born enslaved.[58] This would mean that they could be sold or resold. What an amazing story. I only got to know of this story because of the unveiling of Blue Plaques by the Nubians in the UK, London. Furthermore, Black History Walks and other history lessons are supporting us in reclaiming our heritage and knowing the truth. The Bank of England got its gold from Guinea, West Africa, represented by the gold guinea bearing a tiny elephant; symbolising the ivory trade and the "white gold" of elephant tusks used as trophies by the British army as a symbol of Britishness.[59] So, we can see why this erasing is part of the desire to revive a nostalgic past for the mythical empiric creature, no longer in existence. The inequalities are recognised by the UN and the CEO of the Runnymede Trust Dr. Halima Begum that the UK's, 'Analysis of racial equity is even vaguely feasible.'[60] Similarly, in matters of unseen separation this is what Nickole Hannah-Jones a Pulitzer Prize winner 2020 in investigative journalism of the 1619 Project with *The New York Times* Magazine speaks of extreme deprivation. She seeks to uphold black contribution as a foundation to combat the economic inequalities which may not be apparent.[61] Therefore, our visibility is crucial and protesting is a very powerful way to be present and be seen so that we can be the voice that brings about change at this time of awakening. The paradox is that it appears as if the earth in astrology is going backwards in this Age of Aquarius. This is aligned with the Higher Divine realms to restore creation in the Golden Alchemy through God's plan, the Plan of Love, streaming down from above to the new era earth because, "Love Has Won and his King now rules". This has not necessarily been welcomed particularly by those who wield abusive power that has been taken rather than given in the spirit of goodness as a force for good not conflict or war.

We are always making history not just contributing so I want to get that straight and I hereby, clear the record, that we are makers and shakers of history, history makers. My mission is to elevate this new energy through my vision as a symbolic Owl lighting up my vision board of a better world each day for justice, peace and harmony. Since then, owls are showing up whenever they want. At the same time Africa Is Rising, AIR, "We Can Breathe". This makes her great and her seat of being the country that was chosen for humanity to begin, human life. Therefore, this book with its 3 Rs education is a way of preserving and embodying this narrative of protest for justice, accountability and transparency while symbolising our black or ethnic presence as a living memorial. This book stands in honour of our ancestors and all those who fought for freedom in the past and fight for justice in this present time of awakening and beyond in this unfolding oracle of an evolving era lasting for thousands of years to come.

APARTHEID IN THE EAST

Nelson Mandela words on Palestine is so potent from the image on the front cover because it shows how aware he was on the situation even though he lived through the apartheid regime in South Africa, something that I touch on later on in this book. Mass student protest against the continued genocide in Gaza has spread across US universities from LA to NY despite being harassed by riot police demanding cutting links with Israel and ending arms trade.[1] Universities across the UK took the same stand.[2] According to the Gaza Health Ministry over 35,303 people have been killed including over 15,002 children and over 79,261 have been injured while mass burial sites have been desecrated. The threat of starvation is imminent.[3] In Rafah, families face ground onslaught as gun boats are on the alert.[4] There is carnage. The UN Human Rights calls for Israel to be held accountable for war crimes.[5] South Africa, a country that lived under an apartheid regime brings a case for genocide to the International Court of Justice.[6]

In Westminster young children and their parents protest holding banners and cancelling celebrations for a ceasefire because every 10 minutes is a child's life in Gaza.[7] In the steep stockpile of weaponry over 70 years when as many as 750,000 Palestinians were ousted from Gaza when Israel in 1948 effectively displaced a whole community. The opening up of a market after WWII saw the US become a major investor pumping millions of dollars amounting to over *$124 billion* with the backing of the UK and European investment into a mutated form of trading in people from a colonial past. The Israeli army also live-train US officers and use advance surveillance.[8] The catalyst for this present genocide on Gazans happened on 7 October 2023 when a military group killed over 1,200 people from the Jewish community this atrocity prompting Israel's fiery rational this unthinkable terror on families. I would add that the army is replicating the sufferings of their grandparents transferred onto the Gazans with blood money "assets" in genocide. There are reports from hostages who were at the festival substantiating the fact that it was Israeli helicopters who fired onto their own people.[9] This means that the US and Israel already knew what was going to happen and did nothing to stop it according to Haarterz a Jewish newspaper.[10] Most of the Gazans are refugees living in camps and homes some had built themselves but due to the relentless airstrikes these have become wreckage and a symbol of displacement and the massacre of innocent lives a direct violation on a child's rights to life, to family life.[11] This is based on the United Nations Convention on the Rights of the Child under Article 6. This applies to *all* children to be protected from violence and harm under Article 19.[12] What is the repercussion for violating this convention? The annihilation of families or communities and those who suffer survival anguish used their bare hands to rescue those under the rubble where many cannot be reached over 7,000 people mostly children are still missing; in this human cleansing crime against humanity.[13]

Palestinian rights groups have filed a genocide lawsuit in the US as mass protest against this war on civilian life gathers momentum.[14] Protests have filled the streets in New York, Grand Central Station "Not In My Name", including Jewish Voices for Peace, Bolivia, Djibouti, Yemen, Lebanon, Jordan, Istanbul, Pakistan, Sri Lanka, Bangladesh, Manila, Indonesia, London, Paris, Canada, South Africa and South Korea who laid out shoes for those lost.[15] Those accountable pick and choose inhumanity. The protest has taken place in London every week since the 14 October 2023. On 11 November 2023 a mass protest of over 700,000 people took to the streets of London to voice their indignation including myself.[16] It is no surprise that a good *Christian* country like Britain commemorated Armistice Day on 12 November 2023 simultaneously arming Israel and investing in weapons sent to cause devastation and destruction upon innocence. The largest hospital Al Shifa suffered tanks, shelling, airstrikes, raids and gunfire, eyes closed upon the sick, oblivious to the injured patients and the hundreds of families sheltering with constant shelling, gunfire and mass burials described as a deadly encampment. They trashed specialist equipment while destroying medical supplies needed for the sick.[17] The Al Awda Children's Hospital founded by Dr. Mena EL- Farra lost 44 members of her family through the airstrikes as whole families are wiped out. Not an ounce of empathy or sympathy was shown to her on the televised interview, only an attempt to justify. Her hospital had no pain relief and staff faced intimidation.[18] Schools akin to Fakhoura suffered the same where over 200 people at once lost their lives; mosques and churches sacred sanctuaries were not spared instead these were turned to rubble similar to the rest of the infrastructure. A surgeon from the UK tells his own story about the "terror" of this mammoth shelling siege forlorn on Gaza when he arrived there.[19] They haven't learnt to be human even children are being indiscriminately targeted.

Adam Ghoul, a young boy only 8-year-old was shot in the back while playing with his friend Basil who was also shot by an armed Israeli. His father Samer wished that he was just dreaming.[20] But, he wasn't dreaming, he was fully awake in his grief-stricken pain. A 3-year-old dies of shrapnel, his body in a state of stillness silence, in the street. Basic commodities such as water, food and fuel are being used as missiles as the Gazans and their children face impending starvation.[21] On 17 October 2023, the UN and Doctors Without Borders charity expressed deep concerns that fuel for hospitals was extremely low to the ground.[22] United Nations staff and humanitarian workers or volunteers risk their lives to protect. While those who are not fit to be leaders, as perpetrators and instigators ignore the plight of the families and instead make handshake public relations for camera grapping headlines. Whilst, over 7,800 detainees including children as young as 12 languish in centres unfit for human habitation. My hope is that as long as our humanity remains intact we will conquer all the injustices with the mighty ones above in a moment that will always last and be remembered in a just world.

End Apartheid

Palestine must be Free

Seeing Double

Freedom is Liberation

End the Genocide

Take Back the Occupation

Cease the Fire

STOPPED SEARCHED SHOT OR KILLED

On 27 June 2023 in Nanterre Paris Nahel Merzouk a 17-year-old boy of Algerian and Moroccan heritage was shot dead at point-blank range a bullet accelerating into his chest as he sat in a car. Two officers approached with guns released telling him that they would shoot him in this judge and jury execution.[1] Why were they carrying guns in a residential area to an unarmed situation involving a minor? This made *them* armed and therefore dangerous. This shooting sparked outrage that filled the city for several days of unrest, a video of the shooting went viral on social media. In the US on 7 January 2023 a 29-year-old unarmed black man named Tyre Nichols was sprayed with pepper, tasered, beaten and kicked repeatedly after he was dragged from his car, shown in a video, in Memphis, Tennessee. He was on his way home when he was traffic stopped by five police officers in what has become militarised policing.

He died of his injuries three days later. He just wanted to go home instead he faced the pain of brutal and deliberate violence.[2] This is a time of *Reckoning* over black lives mattering yet still being treated with inhumanity. Protesters expressed their outrage Jon Perry lost his son to this violence expressing through tears, "They wanted him to die." Another young man showed deep scars embedded on his body after a near-death encounter with the police. The protesters want Justice. They want answers. We do too. This is happening daily therefore the media are only reporting a tiny fraction of the scale of black lives not mattering, at the core. The whole of our humanity is at stake due to the fact this "terror" is happening. Why is there an absence of urgency to end *this* terror? One banner reads, 'We Want Justice by Any Means Necessary.' Blood is dripping from their hands with no accountability expressed an activist for the community. Tyre's mother appealed for calm and with incredible courage showed mercy to the officers.[3] A picture of Tyre on Twitter with a beautiful smile reflected his love for skateboarding and nature photography.[4] Had the *George Floyd Policing Act of 2021* been enacted into law a different story might be told here in this narrative where black lives are diminished. The Act would ban neck holds and officers would not be able to claim immunity.[5] Defunding the police is seen as part of the radical change or reforms needed as millions of pounds are poured into policing who are effectively "rewarded" for their crimes. The United Nations working group have been investigating abuse of human rights in the UK and their preliminary research has concluded that Britain's establishments are structurally racist.[6] A documentary looking into why the police targeted and profiled Chris and subsequently killed him in a fatal shooting highlighted the delays the family faced.[7] Chris Kaba died after being trapped inside his car and shot by armed police on 5 September 2022 in Streatham, South London. He was only 24-year-old, unarmed, and was looking forward to becoming a father.

His death triggered a National Day of Action for Justice and the protest march that followed on 17 September put pressure on the police to suspend the officer who opened fire in a residential area.[8] The athlete Ricardo Dos Santos was stopped by police while driving on several occasions also in 2022 because it was thought that he was using his phone. This was not the case and yet 7 *armed* police were called to the scene where he expressed his need to be safe.[9] He had stopped his car in a well-lit residential area after being racially profiled. Fortunately, he had cameras in his car that picked up an officer using his baton, aggressively, hitting the car window. This is another situation of a car stop and what could have had a fatal outcome. They got it wrong, so why would they call for 7 armed police what I call the authorised mob to an unarmed situation wasting resources needed for genuine serious crimes? According to statistics, black males are 40 times more likely to be stopped and searched.[10] The CEO of the charity *The 4Front Project* Temi Mwale, explained that the whole structure on every level has been designed to let down young black males.[11] Boys are being disproportionally excluded from school, racially profiled and incarcerated. According to a poll carried out by GMB 48% of young people, 14-24, say they do not trust the police and 40% say they are racially profiled. Jahnine Davis of the *Listen Up* charity speaks of excessive observation and greater policing and a need to acknowledge racism. Kwajo Tweneboa a campaigner activist voicing how intensely appalled people feel.[12] This is the behaviour of the policing methods and the sheer lack of accountability and transparency. In Hackney, 15-year-old Child Q was stripped and searched in her school based on an unfounded report. The Justice for Child Q protest that followed was a way of calling this out and the outright misuse or abuse of authority. On a much wider scale over 650 children between the ages of 10-17 and 70% who have been stripped searched being boys from 2018 to 2020. This is without safeguarding protocol and human rights considerations under the UNCRC, United Nations Convention on the Rights of the Child.

The point that was being made is how *traumatising* this kind of search is and the fact that 25% of children had no supervision by an appropriate adult such as a parent or guardian. Children's Commissioner for England Dame Rachel de Souza expressed her concern that this is happening.[13] I reiterate that this kind of ethnic targeting should never have gotten started. Moreover, because of the damage it does to community relations families and friends are alienated losing a sense of trust and this means that children can be groomed as they are vulnerable on the streets and cannot turn to those who should be protecting them which puts them in danger. On the streets, younger ones are being accosted; they might be coming from school and are having their bags opened surrounded by one, two, or even three officers. The intensifying stop and search method only serves to alienate a whole community, especially in the use of Section 60 Intelligence where no reason is given. In the US, it emerged in early April 2021 that a young boy Adam Toledo who was only 13 was killed when an officer chasing him opened fire on 29 March

2021.[14] This was the same day as the trial even though his hands were up and clear. Videos showing this were released but this still does not answer the question, "Why as a minor he was shot?" His mother said, "I want the police report."[15] She wants her son's justice. I demand this justice because it could be anyone of ours wherever we are here in the UK, the US or anywhere in the world. I have seen a still of one video but have not watched the actual videos because it just seems so sickening. It makes me wonder, "Is this some kind of pattern, nine minutes of videos still hurting us?" Understandably, a peaceful protest in the community on the West side began for Adam. The crowds were powerful, "Justice for Adam Todelo!" Plus, "Stop Racist Police Terror" "Stop Killing Our Children 48 Hours Cover Up!"[16]

In the US Grand Rapids area, Michigan, Patrick Lyoya a 26-year-old black unarmed man was shot on 4 April 2022 while laying face down on the ground.[17] He is one of over 250 people shot by police this year alone and another 1,000 people between 2020 and 2021. The police must be disarmed because I think they are on a rampage and this is dangerous for our people who live public and private lives. Minnesota again, unbelievably, another killing of unarmed Daunte Wright, only 20-year-old happened when a female officer opened fire while he was in his car on Sunday 11 April 2021. His aunt, Naisha Wright, expressed her sorrow saying, "He didn't deserve to die."[18] He loved and was loved by his family. Civil Rights Activist Reverend Mark Thompson reiterated the fact that, the human rights of black people have been largely ignored. He made the point that whatever the circumstances there are no grounds for a person to be *executed* in an instant.[19] This sense of heartbreaking is actually at the core of our pain sparking more protests and using more force such as the military and curfews. A new historic Bill based on Reparations for African Americans which I hope will have a ripple effect here and around the world is being established now. Taking into account the remnants of slavery and enslavement and the ongoing injustices that impact our community. At the Shiloh Temple International Ministries Church, his mother spoke through tears about when he became a dad and his sense of great joy. At the eulogy Civil Rights Campaigner Al Sharpton expressed dignity; we witness this young one as royal. This deep sense of heartbreak was being felt and echoed as an ongoing heartbreak.[20] Again, the fifth image at the beginning of this book is the beating heart. Our beating heart is keeping us alive, strong and beautiful for thousands upon thousands of years, despite our pain. Yet, they have for a very long time wanted to do away with or break this heart, this endless gift, because it is the only one that keeps on beating for so long. On 23 August 2020 in Kenosha, Wisconsin, the shooting of Jacob Blake 7 times in his back and tasered while his children witnessed this utter violation of his life.[21]

What makes me so indignant is the focus on the aftermath rather than the infliction, I tweeted, 'This officer must face real justice because Jacob was unarmed and trying to end an argument.'[22] This is clear from early reports therefore, I say, "Justice4Jacob". It is a miracle he survived but he may never walk again. Still, he was *chained* to his bed! His father Jacob Blake Sr., said, "He's a human being."[23] The film drama, *Two Distant Strangers* won an Oscar for portraying different scenarios of police brutality toward a young black man. At one point he tries to appeal to this officer's humanity but he has become the bully, with a gun. The question then is, "Who should have their Hands Up?" What struck me at the end was the long list of those who died some of whom were not on the streets but in their homes, even in their beds. They were still not safe.[24] No matter how violent the perpetrators are they expect peace when they know that they intend to cause much suffering. Since 1969 in the UK over 3,180 deaths have occurred in custody, prisons, detention, or immigration centres and also psychiatric wards. The Inquest charity investigates human rights abuses and works with the United Nations Human Rights Office High Commissioner reporting concerns because black people are disproportionately treated differently and that Britain is a structural, racist, institutional country. The inquiry bears this out stressing the urgency for a radical Britain who must go to the roots of its embedded system. Jamar Powell was only 16-year-old *walking* with his four friends in 2020 when he was wrongfully stopped, forced to kneel, handcuffed with a taser at his neck.[25] He was wearing blue jeans, a top and a grey ribbed open jacket yet the description used to stop him is that he was wearing a full black tracksuit running around with a samurai sword! His three friends were also stopped and searched but not their white friend who filmed everything. This outright abuse of power must end now in this time of reckoning. The main officer was still on duty when Jamar's mother brought a civil case that the court upheld. Jamar conveyed his trauma as "seeing" into the depth of his pain.

A Reckoning

BLM PROTEST BRUTALITY

What I witnessed is a history of systemic violence and violation in this video of a much loved black family man named George Floyd showing him being held down by his neck for over 8 minutes by a white officer. His colleagues stood by shielding and aiding this brutality on 25 May 2020 going viral across news and social media. George's last words were, "I Can't Breathe." A harrowing part of this protest, unspoken words, rang out on Saturday 30 May 2020 during mass protest in 25 States across the US from Minnesota, Baltimore, Chicago, California and San Francisco too New York and other cities.[1] This included the UK on the biggest protest on Saturday 6 June 2020 in London and over 260 towns from Birmingham to Sheffield, Manchester to Bristol, Wales and even the Shetlands demonstrating how stirred and mobilised people are in responding to utter violation of rights and dignity.

Protesters ascended upon London, Westminster with righteous indignation for a despicable act of violence. The echoes of, "I Can't Breathe" and chants of George Floyd's name embraced by the BLM *Take The Knee* was very moving; but the "UK is not Innocent" was present. We need to have the same indignation, hungry for justice, here too with over 130,000 activists. Heart radio station pledged to end racism; while the ravaging of covid ran simultaneously, in the heat. Martin Luther King III spoke of "energy" change and the CEO of NAACP Derrick Johnson spoke of a "Different type of culture."[2] I hope that this energy flame keeps on burning, endlessly, because there is such a need for alertness. This living energy is what H.E.R. singer/songwriter spoke about after winning a Grammy for her song, *I Can't Breathe* reiterating the need to keep on carrying the same energy in the struggle.[3] The same kind of sentiments was shared at the service celebration from the Fountain of Praise Church, Houston, Texas, for the man known affectionately as, "Big George". Reverend Al Sharpton, 100 cities Protest, spoke of "Equal Justice" while George's niece passionately expressed her deepest desire for justice to be done for her uncle.[4] A permanent memorial will mark the place of his death to never forget. There is now a Black Lives Matter Plaza in Washington D.C painted in Big Bright Yellow and many other places such as Los Angeles. There are BLM painted in big words in public areas as a reminder so as not to forget and to keep on remembering as a memorial.

After the verdict, his aunt's heartfelt words spoke about how the outcome of the court hearing authenticated the fact that structural racism is real and how we have had to fight against racism for over 400 years.[5] As a tribute to George known as Perry, his aunt spoke of his love that came from his mother and how this love became a passion in all that he lived for in his music, sports and community life. Originally, it was thought that he was held down by his neck for over 8 minutes and 46 seconds; his last words were, "I Can't Breathe."[6]

What has transpired from the proceedings is that the timing was actually 9 minutes and 29 seconds that George was pinned down, equally important, involving three other officers. As an update in 2022, they have been charged in a Federal court with denying George his civil rights to medical care and liberty of unreasonable capture.[7] His son said that the protestors understood his pain when the first trial began with such strong intense emotions for such a family man who was well-loved and missed. Their voices are heard again in defiance of those who do not understand this kind of pain, within our community today. The videos, "What if there wasn't any?" This sent shock waves through the earth. The UK community and the world reacted with the same righteous indignation by taking a stand knowing that being visible means a voice waiting to be heard. One main witness testimony by D.W. was at the scene trying to get the officer's attention saying he saw George, "Struggling to gasp for air" and that he was, "Fading away."[8] Another significant aspect from a key witness, Doctor B.W. Lengenfeld is that George had suffocated or asphyxiated.[9] The police Chief Arradondo stated that George was motionless and handcuffed when force was used and that this was not based on any guiding principles or preparations, instructions, standards or morals.[10] The question then is why has this injustice being allowed to happen? This most important trial must do justice in full that is the only verdict I wanted to hear that will set a precedent as a symbol of justice; though it will never be enough while injustice persist. To add insult to injury those that should lead have the audacity to use the army and have curfews instead of speaking out against violations. The film *Baltimore* tells the story of Freddie Grey who was killed facing downward on the floor at a railway station; he was shot in the back.[11] This kind of brutality is a pattern, a cycle. It creates "news" yes, it is a platform but news particularly black suffering is big business racism and brutality toward countless of our people. Yet, these inhuman acts invoked a massive reaction an extraordinary uprising against the system exclaimed by Professor of Law, Anthony Cook.[12]

Collective Consciousness

Fighting for Equality BLM

Staying Silent Gives Permission

Fundamental: Respect and Dignity

I matter because Black Lives Matter

Red Fiery

Rest in Power & Rest in Peace

The Violence of Silence

The Power of Love Conquers

A child's view, "The UK is NOT INNOCENT."

System Change Now

An Excluding System

This very bold banner indicates that the system is set up or designed in a particular way not fit for the needs of the black community.

Above on the following page there is an equally strong bold message with fewer words. Below a female activist and a young boy fervently chants, "Black Lives Matter!"

Black Lives Matter

Spiriting Justice for George Floyd

End This Now

Deaths in Police Custody

Where is the Justice for them?

The Presence of Self

I am struck by the way pieces of cardboard which would normally be thrown away or recycled are transformed into powerful messages of such individual expressions; thoughts and feelings that are poured into all the different banners.

In this banner the activist uses the letter "I" to signify a very personal self whilst highlighting the deep red blood of those who were victims of police violence or brutality. Also, the "I AM" in the moments of collectiveness identity.

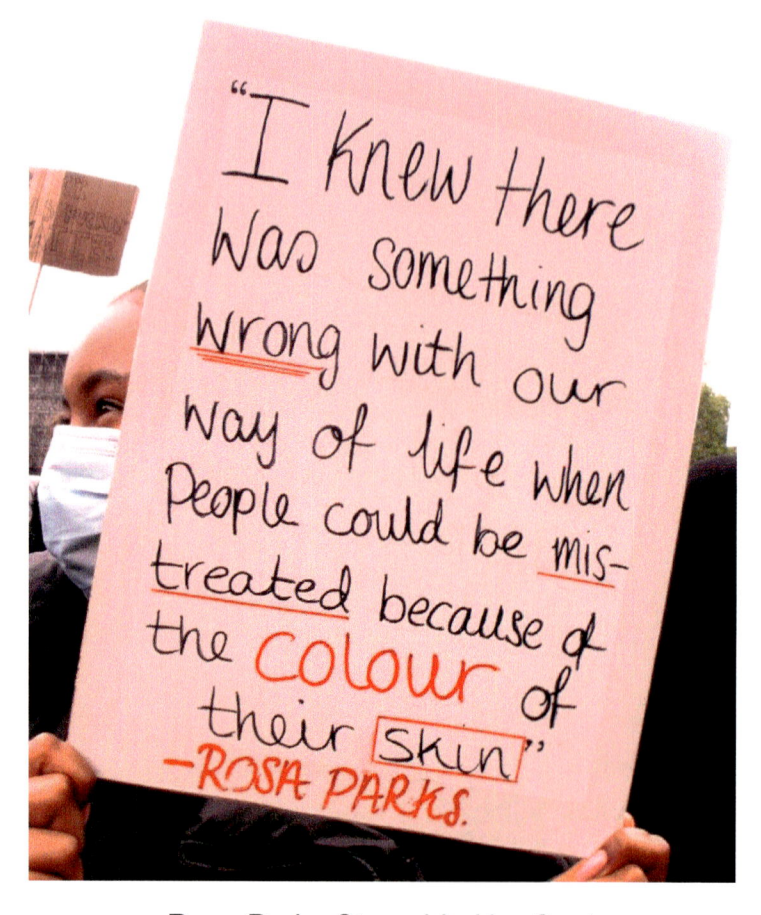

Rosa Parks Stayed In Her Seat

Mother and child hold a banner

A theme in the protest

George's Last Words: "I Can't Breathe."

Say their names, Say their names

Staying Silent Is Lethal

A Family of Friends

Black Lives in Danger

Speak Up for All their Lives

BLM No More Executions

By My Own hand: Black Power Salute

Babylon Will Fall

Our children need their Fathers

White supremacy Must be Eradicated

Hair Discrimination

I Make No Apology

Do you know the answer?

Black Power Black Justice

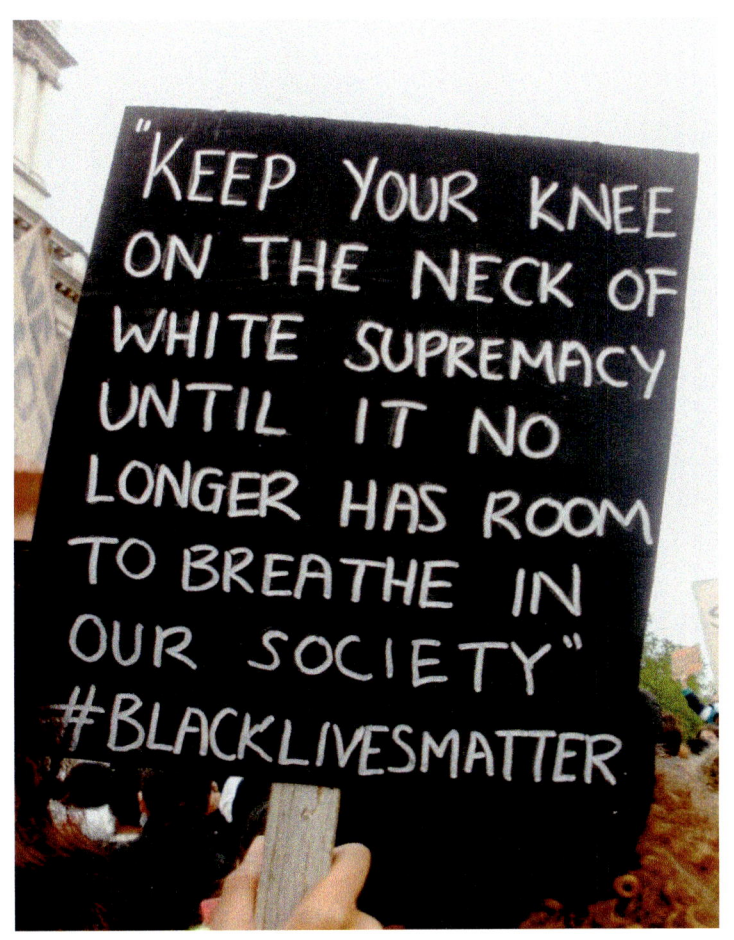

Malcolm X

Breathing

Solidarity

Stop And Search 40 X More in the UK

On the Gates of Westminster

Raise Your Voices

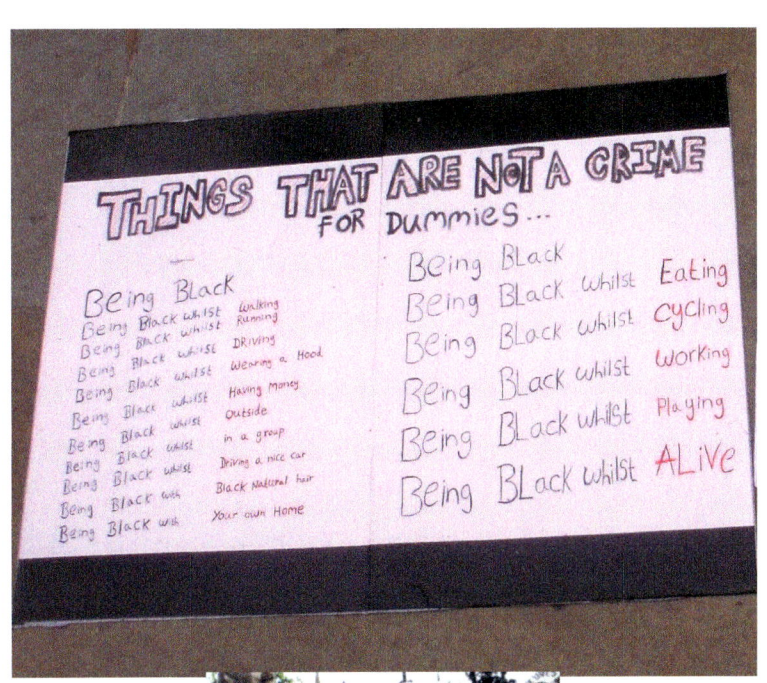

Being Black Whilst Living

Malcolm X Capitalism Needs Racism

Bridge Street SW1: White Silence

Stephen Lawrence Day is 22 April Annually

Rest in Power

The Bigger Pandemic

Black Is Always Beautiful

STAND UP TO RACISM

I totally understand the racism that veteran Diane Abbott MP expressed for which she was punished. Furthermore, attempts to "put her out of service" in the most disgraceful manner for a woman of high calibre, because she made history, was prevented by her sheer bravery and the strength of her campaigners against structural racism[1]. Korrine Sky a medical student who gave evidence to the UN or United Nations in March 2023 stated that guns were held at her group as they tried to escape Ukraine after a Russian invasion. They realised that they were segregated at the border in an attempt to reinforce the myth of some whitening, homogenising culture.[2] In the US on Sunday 15 May 2022 against a backdrop of police violence a heavily armed 18-year-old terror racist opened fire taking the lives of 10 black people. He travelled two hundred miles to a mainly black community in Buffalo, New York, live streaming this shocking atrocity on social media which went viral.[3]

I would suggest that videoing of black suffering is the mutated version of the ancient arena blood sport; it is the *spectacle* in the media, to win the crowd. On 24 February 2022 when war broke out in Ukraine in the last week through a Russian invasion people started fleeing to other countries such as Poland, across the border with Ukraine. But, African students were victimised and assaulted by the Ukranian military. Another student Benibo express her pain of being whipped and beaten and thrown of trains by a racist army.[4] Miss Otto expressed the same sentiments that they would priorities white people first.[5] This oppressive history, this legacy, its repercussions right here even in the freezing temperatures. This was the same story on social media African families were denied access to a haven not being allowed to enter Poland or Hungary without needing a visa. Marcus Ryder a journalist representing the Centre for Diversity in Media voicing the need for equality for everyone.[6] Over 82 million people are already displaced and 450 million children live in conflict zones according to Save the Children 2022 and United Nations High Commission UNHCR for Refugees. Boys are at risk of becoming soldiers and women are violated. Why aren't there the same sentiments for them across the news media? This is selective inhumanity at its very core. Syrian refugees of 6.8 million and others fled from war-torn countries.[7] Here in the UK Parliament is putting through its Nationality and Borders Bill a callous and inhuman attitude spilling over into a plan to send some refugees to Rwanda 4,000 miles away. Steve Valdez-Symonds from Amnesty calls this, "A despicable policy." Fortunately, the European Courts on Human Rights, ECHR, swiftly intercepted this plan just in time but it can still happen though tagging is the new option...refugees to be treated like criminals. New laws are being introduced to send "migrants" back to their country without the right to claim asylum. While deportations including 74-year-old Lewin William a Jamaican man with cancer was due to take place.[8]

As expressed during the 2020 protest, "The UK is NOT INNOCENT!" On 2 June 2021 'A talented young boy' 14-year-old Dea-John Reid was killed before being taunted by race hate including the "N-word". The community in Birmingham was extremely concerned reporting the incidents to the police.[9] They didn't take it seriously as race hate or question whether the racists themselves had criminal records. They were acquitted by an all-white jury urging the family to campaign for changes to the law in terms of having a diverse and varied jury from many different backgrounds and experiences. On Sunday 23 May 2021 Sasha Johnson, a member of BLM in London was shot having previously been targeted. I retweeted, 'How hateful someone could be to do this to a beautiful black woman willing to challenge and fight for our rights. They didn't even think of her children.'[10] How could this happen? She is stable but has "catastrophic" injuries and no justice but her mum hopes she will tell her story one day.[11] Sasha has been bedridden for over a year now and she is going heal gradually.

As Black Studies Professor Kehinde Andrews at the University of Birmingham, echoed in conversation at a live Zoom event, "The world depends on racism."[12] I think same that racism is not an isolated incident it is global but ours is the longest and the deepest, "The one story" says Lemn Sissay, the award-winning poet, coming out in the midst of the covid lockdowns.[13] The late sporting hero legendary footballer Pelé passed away on 29 December 2022. He became famous for his special gift as a footballer taking Brazil to three World Cups. In the struggle he stood for the rights of black people. He was looked upon with royalty and given a military ceremony and there was great celebration in the streets.[14] The atrocious blatant overt racist rhetoric after England's football final toward young black players Rashford, Saka and Sancho were targeted on social media. The booing at the *Take The Knee* in the stadium in reality exposed how racism is authorised even though there are campaigns to Kick Racism Out of football.

The footballers showed their fearlessness in taking the fight from the pitch to the rich to those that ought to be leading this country. The support, especially in Manchester homing Rashford's mural which was defaced by the debased; though, many people cared enough to take a stand with a protest gathering for BLM. However, the idea that only a couple of people are racist is quite common thinking that racism is not a depiction of our world a version of the world we exist in.[15] In fact, it is according to psychologist John Amaechi. He also makes the point that racism can seem stylish or trendy, rather than based on class. The inside story of overt racism within the covert world of the monarchy is exposed when the shade of the skin colour of Meghan Markle's baby is seen as an issue before he was even born.[16] This micro-aggressive undercurrent sent shock waves reverberating in the US and UK and the onslaught of tabloid vilifying in its menacing nature toward a vulnerable woman of colour. Then this silence before and after in this instigated and "perpetrated racism" says Dr Shola Mos-Shogbaminu. The well-known barrister Shola Mos-Shogbaminu received death threats on 22 February 2023 from a right-wing fascist group known in the UK. Shola is known for being outspoken and standing against racism. Understandably, although fearful for her family she remained steadfast in voicing black rights of belonging in the UK.[17] Knowing that without us, they wouldn't exist. It is also about the rhetoric or language that is fuelling racism embedded in the whitening homogenising system. Moreover, any report that denies institutional systemic racism is creating a missed opportunity for reform in this white *privilege* system. It is extremely damaging and dangerous to absolve those who are accountable and who should face justice so that they are not on the streets or going into people's homes. This includes erasing over 20 years of admission from Dr. R. Oakley in the Stephen Lawrence Inquiry a, '*systemic tendency that could unconsciously influence police performance.*'[18]

There is this sense of unwittingly though my view is that there is a culture of unaccountability, immunity, instead of choosing to do the right thing. Policing is a publicly funded service involving taking an oath to protect and serve and they did neither not even give first aid and proper care to Stephen. The 22 of April, has become the Stephen Lawrence Day and it was comforting to think of his life and the impact that he had at such a young age and is still having on the lives of younger ones, his legacy.[19] There is a beautiful mural to his name in Hackney, East London.

My experience that I think is a trend was during a hospital consultation when I was asked, "Are you foreign?" I was stunned and pained. There was no reason given for this first consultation question only noting my birth status and needless to say I challenged this unethical and racial discriminatory approach. I knew that had I been white I would not have been asked the *question*. However, rather than an admission I got what I call justified rationalisation where the reasons given to know one's ethnic origin appears to be in the best interest of the patient instead of a slippery slope, two-tier, healthcare system. Another example is the concept of "psychological passing". It concerns what is called, "Shopping While Black" and like myself being racially profiled while shopping; scrutinised or observed. In fact, my experience was almost identical to Amoah the CEO of Backlight.[20] Thus, making shopping an uncomfortable experience to say the least with the increasing surveillance, without consent.

The housing crisis is another arena of discrimination and this means that the home is not necessarily a place of comfort. Kwajo Tweneboa is a young black male housing campaigner on a mission to bring major change; the experience of his dad and himself in social housing was appalling and he became very concerned about conditions in the social housing sector. Some of these are leaks, collapsing ceilings, dampness, mould, mice, inadequate repairs and racial discrimination. This is what I call a scandal in the housing sector. He stressed the need for more housing and voiced that racism and unfavourable treatment is unquestionably an aspect within community housing.[21] My own situation with impact and airborne noise nuisance due to flooring plus major water damage, damp, mould and cracking ceilings. This is *statutory* negligence by my local council to safely enjoy my home. This combines with a neighbour whose kids treat the place like a playground. This local authority in their heartlessness "Smile up in front of the cameras!" They claim to look after their residents simultaneously trying their hardest to make properties uninhabitable and thereby induce a social cleansing, disgraceful.

93

Mould in Sleeping quarters

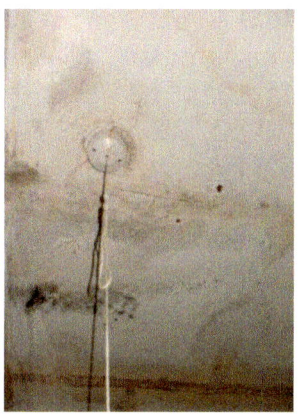

Water Damage Mould

The *Stand Up To Racism* online protest on 22 May 2021 exposed the extent of the racism and the need to keep on Standing Up and call it out. It was painful to listen to the attendees and hear their stories their traumas and sufferings and their determination to challenge these injustices in the system, which needs a radical change at its foundation; voiced Zainab Hassan whose nephew was killed and still the family have no true answers. Ryan Colaco was targeted, handcuffed and interrogated by the police who also damaged his car but were cleared by the CPS who believed in their deceit. This is an absolutely disgraceful service toward members of the public. Those men should have been held fully accountable stripped of their uniforms and unceremoniously discharged paying for damages in compensation including emotional and hence, physical pain which is racial trauma.

The Reverend Kobi Little representing the National Association of the Advancement of Coloured People, NAACP, spoke of government endorsement of hate and a "spiral of violence" while global protest is sustained against this outrage. Councillor Anna Rothery's reiterated to keep on fighting for the sake of our humanity. Many of the attendees were young adults and I was impressed and saddened by their speeches. Andrew Boateng was stopped and searched while biking with his son shaking him to the core leading him to campaign for human rights. In the campaign for justice the Free Siyanda Campaign Appeal began. Lawrence Davis welcomed the inquest into the death of Belly Mujinga, a long time coming. Diane Abbott MP reiterated that the State death of George Floyd went global and by the same on 25 May 2021 we *Take The Knee* again. [22] Mohammed Rashir spoke about his family's pain for his brother. On 16 March 2019 thousands marched as part of the United Nations Day of the Elimination of Racial Discrimination in London and globally around the world. This came a day after a mass shooting on 15 March inside a mosque in Christchurch, New Zealand. So many innocent people were killed or injured in this mindless act of hate.

Eliminate Racism

Solidarity is Togetherness

"Lucy" is one of the oldest humans found in Ethiopia

Teaching the Child what is Good

No Staying Silent Anymore

Provide Safe Passages

Music The One Language

End Hostility Now

COVID UNCOVERED

Over 7,006,971 people have lost their lives to covid worldwide with the US being 1,219,487 and 232,112 people in the UK from families.[1] In the UK an inquiry called the UK Covid-19 Inquiry is underway looking into the handling of covid. The main inquiry took place in January, February and March 2023. Members of the public can share their experiences anonymously online.

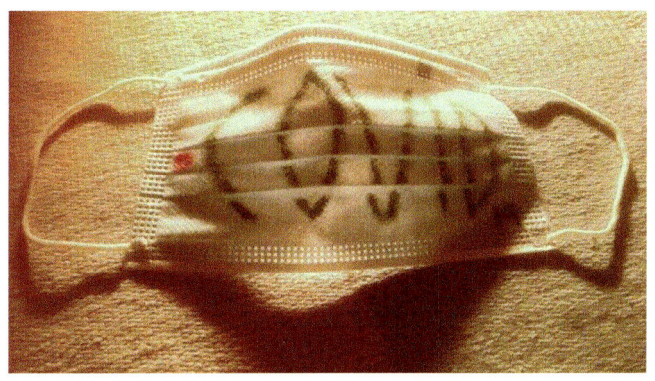

A basic surgical mask worn by millions globally

Since early October 2022 an inquiry into the handling of the covid pandemic has been set up that is so important because many families have been impacted by it and hence there are questions about accountability.

Lobby Akinnado, is one family representing the Covid 19 Bereaved Families for Justice whose father Femi died as a result of not having the protection as a frontline worker.[2] There have been some recommendations made however it all depends on whether these are followed and put into action to protect lives. Furthermore, my view is that the families should also be compensated for emotional and financial considerations. Covid rather than disguise or equalise the inequalities has actually blown them out of the very water. The point I want to make here is that although the NHS is very diverse this does not equate with actual equality. Covid has shown up the inequalities even more than pre-2020. Black and minority groups make up over 40 per cent of NHS workers but this is not reflected in the top *position* as Dr. Amir Khan who is a GP in Leeds admits the "missed opportunity" that there are large proportions of inequalities based on racial grounds that needs to be addressed. He goes on to talk about the structural racism found and reinforced within the NHS. [3]

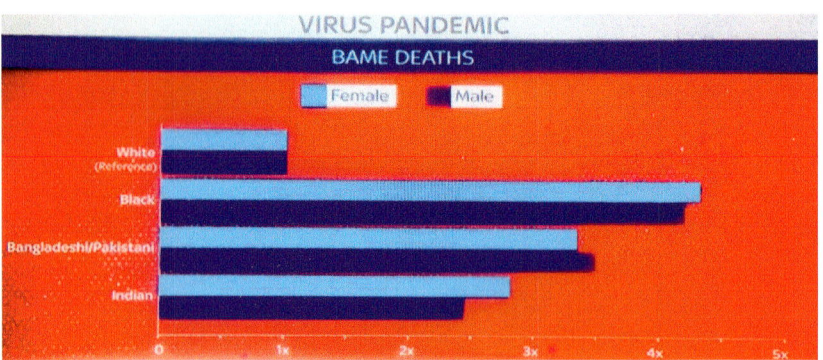

Data from Office of National Statistics 2020

The chart from the Office of National Statistics above shows the risk to black communities was more than 4 times the population.[4] In the "herd immunity" this amount from our communities in the NHS is an extraordinary number and being from this background makes me realise just how much this country is dependent upon black and ethnic labouring in what is an institution. In the UK about a third of all the fatalities from covid have had a devastating effect on black and minority communities in particular without any apology. Covid is already part of the system and that is why it is exposing what needs to be exposed even more because it is time to do what needed to be done and you will find more about this in my next chapter. According to audit research of ICU, Intensive Care Units, 34% of all the intensive care patients were from Black or Asian groups, disproportionately, prompting further research for data commissioned by the Chief

Rainbows of Hope

Medical Officer for Public Health England.[5] Still, there is this attitude that it couldn't be due to any discrimination because that's already in the system without actually grasping what is staring them in the face the discriminatory nature and practices underlying all the institutions that exist and this is what covid has shown up with its forms of mutations and this is just in the UK alone.

Other factors such as historical legacies of deprivation or poverty and the impact on health such as diabetes, high blood pressure, fibroids, sickle cell anaemia and poor maternity care highlighted by the charity *5 X More* showing black women are more at risk especially during childbirth and I think the lack of empathy and engaging with our community means that even access let alone treatment is a real concern. This is neglect and an appalling NHS service. A leading doctor from the BMA, British Medical Association, Dr Nagpaul spoke out about the number of NHS and social care staff dying from the covid and when this was brought into the briefing arena it was like dodging the issue with this does not discriminate kind of tone in answer to the questions raised.[6] The question to ask then is, "Were the *right* people on our side?" What really struck me about the personal stories of the families is how many were from black backgrounds and I realised that this was the only time I had ever seen so many black people from the black community through the media in this context in the UK. The risk factor to our community back then was over 4 X more and therefore I am thinking, "Our people were at risk on the frontline and not even got their PPE" or Protective, Personal, Equipment. Even worse, having to use bin liners as protection now deemed as unlawful.[7]

They were out there and there was no real urgency to protect them under the Equality Act of 2010, as an ethnic community. This was not our battle.   This war-willed without weapons was theirs and yet our people are being sacrificed again. Somehow, taking a pill is not going to cut it! The underlying inequalities must be addressed now as part of Reparations here in the UK and the US, Caribbean and Africa and other parts of the world where black people live.   Instead of heroines and heroes this situation shows that our front-line workers deserved protection. There must be justice and accountability for the families I would say that, "We are living in a state of mutation for far too long and now is the time for truth and justice". Therefore covid becomes the teacher, teaching us what the most important things are at this time of human renewal and how it is possible to live in an entirely different way than what is considered to be normal which is necessary for real lasting change to be realised in our lifetime.

REPARATIONS MARCH

This is the sixth Reparations March on 1 Mosiah or 1 August 2019, Brixton, London. The theme is, 'Education is Preparation for Reparations' and this means what we are learning and remembering about ourselves from our ancestral roots is the foundation for knowing where we are going in terms of fighting for what belongs to us. I expressed on 16 August 2019, "Our people were never slaves". At the Black Cultural Archives in Brixton, presented by Professor Hakim Ali, Historian/Pan-African that is why they fought for their freedom. But, they were *enslaved* in a Black Holocaust and we still are by an oppressive system. Colonialism, especially in the race for Africa, just shifted the plantations into the mutated version of slavery which abounds today. More resources are coming out of Africa than what is going in even with aid support because of the high interest on loans, control of resources, diamonds, oil, trading and UK waste.

The West must cancel all debt because they are the ones that *owe* Africa and this is part of the reckoning. It is public knowledge that chocolate companies namely Nestle have their headquarters in Geneva of all places and Cadburys established by Quaker enslavers despite being a "Christian" religion. What about the major churches' masquerade and their enslaved, whitening, history? There is now a consensus from public opinion calling for an apology and financial reparations toward the major institutions to act.[1] St Paul's hosted an event to discuss racial issues as part of Black History Month in October 2019 and what stood out was the silence in predominately white churches and this point that pastor Ben Lindsay voiced that needs to be said in these churches that they stand against racism and show this actively in their words and deeds.[2] I watched the screening of the *Empire Pays Back*, with Robert Beckford, in 2005. In 2023, the Brattle report states that Britain owes the descendants *£18 Trillion* in reparations justice.[3] In addition, the biggest payout at that time to the enslavers about £16 billion today.[4] Therefore, we are now

The Horrors of Slavery

charging for genocide, menticide, and ecocide collectively called Maangamizi a Swahili word and we demand the inquiry now from our protest call on 1 August 2019 and hereafter. Illinois, Evanston in Chicago is the first place that *Reparations* money is being paid out to black residents in recognition of damage, racial divide and, "Crimes against the humanity of Black people" says Robin Rue Simmons for community representation.[5] On the surface this may seem the start of a kind of repairing However, there are conditions attached that involve buying up run-down houses that might not sell. There should not be any conditions none at all. However, system discrimination, racism and its legacy are at the core but trillions of dollars are printed says activist Marlon Watson. To them I say, "Print the money!" What about the UK? There does seem to be this idea especially by those who gained the most from slavery, similar to Britain, that it is just this "stain". If only, Britain could just wash this stain away with its whitening soap it could just pretend that slavery never even happened despite the fact that the descendants still carry the surnames of their enslavers and the sheer scale of this oppressive human legacy.

Black Freedom Fighters

Redeeming the Past

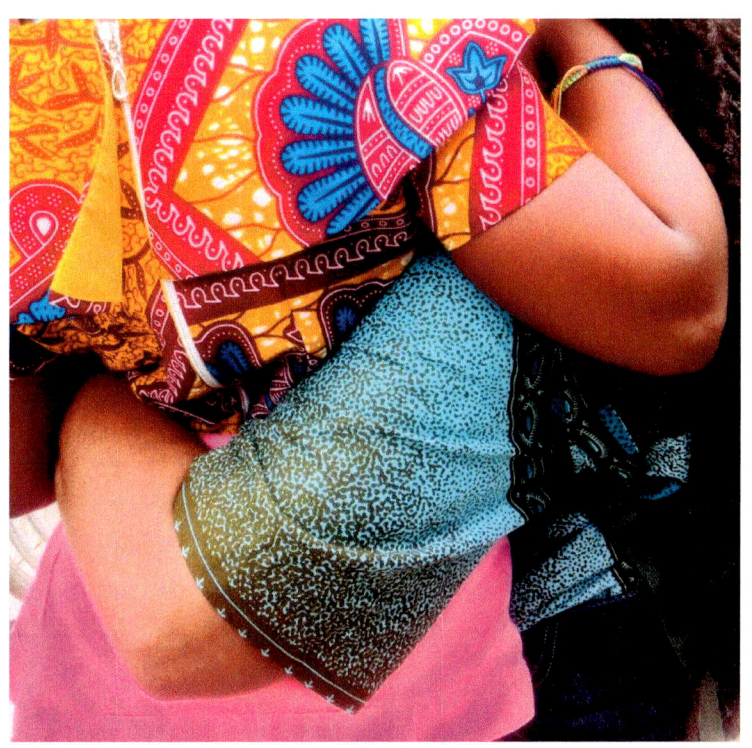

Embracing Mother and Child

Sacred Ritual

Drumming the Heartbeat of Tradition

Calling it Out

Marching for Reparations

Honouring Our Ancestors

A crowd full of Joy

Warriors African Women

The Legend of Bob Marley

Africa in Red Gold and Green in the Black Salute

The Greatest Muhammad Ali

Fire, Fire

Tambourine the March

We Are Resourceful

"Liberty, Liberty, Liberty!"

UNITED FAMILIES & FRIENDS CAMPAIGN

The United Families & Friends Campaign Rally began in Trafalgar Square to Whitehall on Saturday, 27 October 2018 since 1998.[1] "What do we want?" The crowd responding:

"Justice!"

Truth is JUSTICE

"When do we want it?"

"Now" replied the powerful voices of a crowd not dissuaded by the very cold weather. Families took turns to speak passionately about the unbelievable injustices to an attentive crowd. I took care of the banner for Seni Lewis for a while, *11* police officers restrained him.[2] What I call weight weapon and using a stunt gun to debilitate him, showing the cowardice of the policing methods. I spoke with Mark Duggan's family he was unlawfully shot by police. I remember seeing the actual screening of this on the television and it was definitely a chase, like a hunt. The *4WardEver Campaign* marked 40 years of the Brixton protest in 1981 in their 81 Acts of Exuberant Defiance events which I joined online in the UK 2021.[3] The 1981 Uprisings is seen as an important moment of mass rebellion across the country. I call this time a "Collective Act of Indignation" against an oppressive system that exploded onto the streets of Brixton with a major civil rights protest of 15,000 on 2 March from New Cross to Westminster because thirteen were dead and nothing was said...

Policing: No Safety No Protection

We Demand Justice

Trauma

Brutal Mental Health

Justice for Seni

Justice for Sean

BLM

Expressions of Pain

Fighting for Transparency

Fighting for Accountability

Temi Mwale the CEO of the 4Front Project

Family members and friends United for Justice

Nuno Deserves Justice

Words of Wisdom

State Sanctioned Violence is a Crime

WINDRUSH BETRAYAL

The Windrush betrayal highlighted the fact that many of the Windrush generation who came here as babies, children or young adults still found themselves subject to *hostile* immigration policies going back to the 1950s which included being deported or detained in immigration centres.[1] The compensation payout is very slow relying on the victims to show how they have been affected for support from the £260 million for over 15,000 survivors. Even worse, being denied NHS care or pay extortionate payments for health or documentation as proof; landing cards allegedly done away with in stark contrast to EU settlement.[2] Thus, opening the floodgates to European settlement within the UK. Were Polish landing cards destroyed?

During the 1970s immigration status changed and so did citizenship. This is what Anthony Brown found when in his 20s he wanted to study here. He is now a lawyer helping other sufferers.[3] In 1948, around 492 people from the West Indies came on the Windrush ship to Tilbury, England. Some were RAF service persons on board that had actually departed but arriving back. The 1948 Nationality Act conferred full citizenship rights. But, by 1971 those rights were revoked yet the labouring power meant that Britain had a chance to rebuild being on its knees. Hubert Howard was one of many thousands in Britain for over 59 years and who was still treated like an illegal immigrant before citizenship was finally granted to him.[4] The Windrush March on 22 June 2019 from Whitehall rallying through to Parliament and Westminster Bridge marked a Protest in support of over 50,000 persons who have been denied their citizenship rights. Hence, the Windrush March expresses the sheer unbelievable treatment of the Windrush generation who have lived here even more than 50 years being *stripped* of their British identity. We stopped traffic not to forget. A ruling made on 25 November 2020 stated that the Home Office ignored section 149 of the Equality Act 2010, by the Equality Human Rights Commission in the UK.[5]

The Legal Challenge

Black and Strong

Fighting for All Windrush

A View Through The Lens

"We were taught to love the 'Mother Country' only to find out that our mother doesn't love us"

Quote from conversation with Brent community

REMEMBERING GRENFELL

The third and fourth memorials were during the lockdown restrictions so there was an online event instead. I lit a large candle and used bell ringing from Oxford. These images are from the Grenfell Wall under the Tower that I took for the first time on June 14, 2019. In the evening there was a gathering outside near the local church as, earlier in the day, there was a memorial service for the families who lost loved ones.

The outdoor service was so intimate, moving, soulful, solemn, yet powerful with this amazing poem, children's choir and heartfelt singing. Stormzy in green was once again present in the evening. A young man who lost his friend was writing as I took an image he started off with similar to, 'In the name of God...' Also, I got talking with a lady who is Ethiopian from the writing on the wall and we just hugged each other. Grenfell's inquiry highlights the fact that key witnesses were avoiding coming forward. Described as "gutless cowards" by Edward Duffarn of Grenfell United and Karim Mussilhy who said that the makers of the inflammable cladding, "Knew that their products were dangerous."[1] So knowingly, they went ahead cladding the Tower.

A Special Peace for Grenfell

In the Name of God

Written in native Ethiopian

A Heart full of Roses

A Teddy holds a Single Rose

Just One Question, "Why?"

Endless

Grenfell United

Paying Respects Latimer Road

COMMONWEALTH WAR MEMORIAL

Britain's new Head of State means that the countries of the Commonwealth will decide through campaigning for independence or autonomy their right to govern. The timing of politicians meeting delegates from the Caribbean Commonwealth in May 2018, during the height of the Windrush betrayal, was a complete embarrassment for the UK which is an understatement.

Caribbean and African Regiments during WWI & II

Yet, in Brixton's Windrush Square stands a Memorial near the Black Cultural Archive Museum, London. Although, I am part of a living memorial, this memorial evoked such emotions in me; revealing my African heritage stretching back into Britain even beyond pre-Roman times. The long campaign as a protest honours those especially from Africa and the Caribbean their efforts recognised at last at great cost. Over 165,000 men came from parts of Africa with the impact of an impoverishing effect felt in much of Africa which demands independence from the West.

Honoured and Remembered

Sacrifice for a Country Unworthy

"The African and Caribbean War Memorial was created by Nubian Jak Community Trust in partnership with the West Indian Association of Service Personnel and supported by the Heritage Lottery Fund. Lambeth Council, the Black Cultural Archives and Madstone Ltd"

Nubians the Early Pharaohs

MANDELA

"THE STRUGGLE IS MY LIFE"
NELSON MANDELA
GAOLED 5th AUGUST 1962
SENTENCED TO LIFE IMPRISONMENT
12th JUNE 1964 FOR HIS ACTIONS
AGAINST APARTHEID

ERECTED BY THE GREATER LONDON COUNCIL
UNVEILED BY OLIVER TAMBO
PRESIDENT OF THE AFRICAN NATIONAL CONGRESS
28th OCTOBER 1985

NELSON MANDELA WAS RELEASED
AFTER 27 YEARS' IMPRISONMENT

Bust of Nelson Mandela 1985

As if by chance, I learnt about Nelson Mandela's exhibition at the Southbank, in London, July-August 2018, the centenary of his birth 18 July, 1918 and it was wonderful to learn more about the child, the youth, the man, named Nelson by the British colonial regime trying to erase his African cultural heritage. He grew up realising as I have that he was living under a growing oppressive regime. He knew that something radical had to happen. This meant great sacrifices for him, his friends and his family who didn't get to live as normal a life. But, he knew that what had become "normal" under apartheid was not what he envisioned and he sought to bring about change devoting himself, to his life.

Losing Freedom to gain a new Freedom

He lost his physical freedom but gained a spiritual one through this process of incarceration on Robben Island, where he learnt to use his resources to become the person to lead his country.

Of course, this has not brought about the kind of equality and end of poverty that he envisioned because the dynamics are complex, deep and structural not just political or military but part of much wider issues involving previous colonial countries and their histories that we demand reparations justice at a time that is calling for the debt of the slave trading and it's legacies to be settled.

Nelson Mandela unjustly imprisoned for 27 years

Awarded the Noble Peace Prize in 1993

I was able to get a glimpse of him as a child at school who became a famous freedom prisoner and the gradual process of how his experiences changed his outlook. His struggle against a brutal apartheid regime was projected onto a screen showing the military regime inflicting their brutal violence against innocence in a massacre of school children.

On display, was his school eagle badge, Xhosa tribe family tree, ceremonial bridal beads, family visit list, his notes from literature writings or books, his tool from hard labour, images of the protest to free him and his fellow comrades incarcerated on Robben Island. He came to the UK in 1962, 1996 and 2008 and was received and welcomed as the Statesmen he became; he also met music artists such as Stevie Wonder, Diane Ross, Michael Jackson and Oprah Winfrey. I wasn't aware of all this campaigning in the 1980's due to trauma. However, I did get to watch the live screening when Mandela walked free as the statesman he became and there was just this sense of jubilance and the crowds that gathered had to see him for themselves. It was a moment in history when he had become a history maker.

PATRISSE AND ANGELA AT WOW

As part of the International Women's Day I listened to Patrisse Khan-Cullors, "No more" in terms of harassment, violence and silence on stage at the WOW, Women of the World, festival 9 March 2018. She is NAACP, History Maker and the co-founder of BLM, Black Lives Matter. The organisation came into being as a force for social justice in response to racism, police violence or brutality and became a mass movement around the world.

Los Angeles, she's a Fulbright scholar, and making history.

A Maker of History

It has many principles such as engagement, empathy, diversity, collectiveness and restoration in creating change as well as campaigning. I was able to capture some images with live captions of what led to establishing the Movement showing how there is systematic mutation of oppression and the need to demand true Abolition not just the transatlantic version of a stolen people but freedom and *rights*. It was amazing to have renowned iconic activist Angela Davis, in conversation at the WOW festival in London, on 8 March 2019. She said that, "Individualism is the great problem of our times." Although, I think this might be changing because of our collective conscious mind.

I'm just wondering how whether that was the engine for coming up with this incredible movement that you co-founded.
PATRISSE: Yeah, well hi London. Yes.

PATRISSE: Yeah, well hi London. Yes. Represent. It's really good to be here, I just want to take a moment to give gratitude and yeah. Just whenever I'm on these stages it is nice to look around and see who

Welcome London

was a real live debate and it was infuriating because black people knew racism wasn't over and that a single black President wasn't going to era so500 years and then Trevor Martin is killed and then we witness a

Racism Deeply Entrenched

allow George zimmer man to have the period to the story. He wasn't going to be able to walk out of that courtroom and go home and sleep that night without us raising hell. Black Lives

No More Getting Away

BLACK LIVES MATTER

The 100 cities marched against injustice when teenager Trayvon Martin, a minor, was gunned down on 26 February 2012, coming back from the sweet shop. I marched in 2013 and my banner image is included.[1] In the UK, I witnessed the power of the youthquake. My heartfelt poem of storytelling in traditional culture fervently expresses One 2 Many. Instead of captions my poem speaks. BLM US now have a Right to Know Bill, in 2018, for transparency and public access which we demand in the UK and across the world because injustice spreads just like wild fire.

In the summer of June and July 2017, four young Afro Caribbean men Darren, Shane, Edson and Rashan, only 20-year-old, killed on 22 July; fathers brutalised and racially profiled by police in Coventry, Leicester, Stratford and Kingsland Road, Hackney.[2] My heartfelt indignation. My tweet said, "We have to take a stand for JUSTICE and voice our utter indignation for injustices so that those in positions are ACCOUNTABLE to the LAW."[3] In Baton Rouge in the US, on 5 July 2016 Alton Sterling was gunned down outside a shop. On 10 July 2016 the chants of "Black Lives Matter" rang out here and in the US, Saint Paul, Minnesota in protest when on 6 July Philando Castile was fatally shot while sitting in his car with his partner and his child with him.[4] Still, they didn't care despite their vows to serve and protect the public in a way that they deserve to be treated with both dignity and respect.

BLM for Trayvon

Words of Malcolm X

Asian Solidarity

US Embassy End Police Terror

ONE 2 MANY

One 2 Many this is what I must voice

we know the truth you are making your choice.

The reality is it's a time to be strong for in

hiding a beast takes its place among thorns.

Our power galore we rise before long

yet hunted, shot, execution style.

Why have you left the innocent to die?

We shout, "Hands up, don't shoot!" Still our

men are dead nothing said from the

top just grassroots instead.   Our ancestors,

tribes, empower our words, words that get

treated as if their unheard. When will you

hear us and open your eyes?

I guess, you would rather believe in your lies.

"No justice no peace!" We shout loud and clear
this time don't say you're not able to hear.
You are accountable before God and me
But, you think you've gotten away scot free.
Know this, in the moment you think you are safe
be sure to envision your most silent fate...
do something redeeming, before it's too late.

Black Lives Matter be blessed my men,
sons, fathers, sistars you are greater than them.
Flying high above the realms of this earth
looking down as angels perceiving our worse.
Sacred your spirits that shine pure as light
please fill our world with justice so bright
shining your beacons in the cold, dark, of night.

Global Justice

GRENFELL ONE YEAR ON

It is one year on from when the unthinkable emerged a fire not seen since the Blitz swept through Grenfell Tower, in Kensington and Chelsea, the richest borough taking the lives of 72 people. I came again to the place and stood with many people where a fervent and young emotional speaker caught my attention. He had a strong, powerful voice he just captivated everyone. Later, I spoke with different people a young lady originally from California, fire-fighters who rescued families, friends sitting together, a person from Liverpool, another originally from India.

Three Hearts

A parent allowed me to take photos of her children just being in the unity was such a wonderful feeling of togetherness. The choir sang again this time at the foot of the Tower; it was incredible to see children even babies, girls, boys, youth, women, men and even pets all wearing the colour green. I could feel that this was a real community spirit and so much was provided – a massive pot of food, rice, drinks, music and song. Movingly, a lady soprano sang *Ave Maria*. We walked silently passing a long wall of hearts then going down a road I lived in as a child toward a tribute park. Quickly, the park became filled with families and many people stood outside to listen knowing that being there mattered to us.

A Rainbow of Love

For the Children

For the Teachers

Capitalism Is Cuts

A safe and stable Nest

The Truth Must be Told

Wearing Green for Grenfell

You Are Light

A Day to Remember: 14 June 2017

From my beginning I am till now

I am free as I go beyond the Skies

GRENFELL REMEMBRANCE WALLS

During the time of writing and narrating through imagery of this book a harrowing atrocity took place in London a tower called Grenfell in North Kensington, West London, caught fire in the 27 storey flats around 12.40am on 14 June 2017.[1] Residents were very concerned about safety issues, about 19, which were ignored by a tenant management who acted obliviously. Lives were put at risk and much suffering and lost that could have been prevented if only the families had been listened to attentively. A young man was saying that there were no-go areas and I deeply sensed a big divide with over 1,300 empty homes despite the housing crisis. A micro mutated version of land enclosures which began centuries ago as part of the feudal hierarchy system of land ownership.

I was so moved by the community spirit when I visited the site and the community coming together in such a loving, caring, human way despite the lack of official help as usual. Many families were distraught. But, the sheer scale of this atrocity, is an act of violence against such beautiful ones. Those responsible who are accountable and must be brought to justice have tried to rip the very heart out of a close-knit community, a desecration. There truly are no words to describe the absolute inhumanity and the images I took of the Remembrance Walls, will stay in this book in memory of the innocent ones who were sacrificed for profit, now forever eternal. Families living in their community should have been able to feel a haven a place for them to bring up their families; in one of the richest countries, fifth in the world, in the *richest* borough in the Capital in the UK. This divide between rich and poor now so poignant a modern day mutated feudal system. If this tower block housed the rich millionaires it would have had the best quality of materials and extra fire safety costing millions from within the building. Instead, the aesthetics outside of the tower was the priority rather than the inside living spaces for families to feel safe and secure enjoying their homes.

The Truth of the Matter

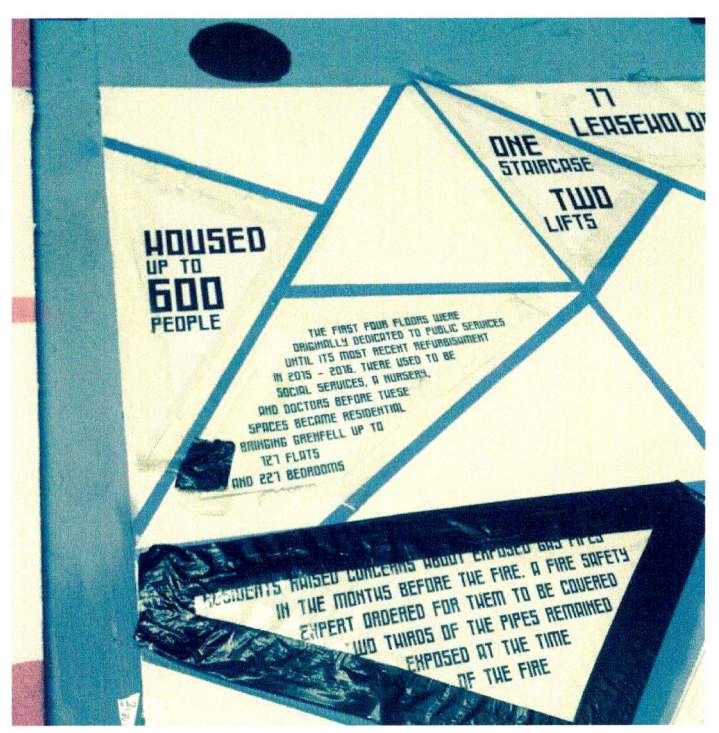

Exit route for 600 people

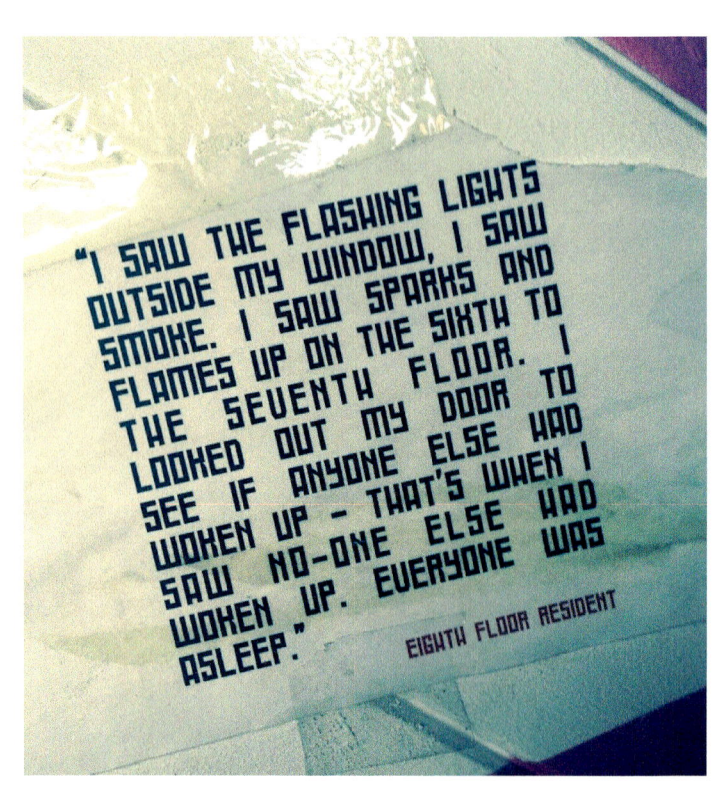

Grenfell on June 14, 2017

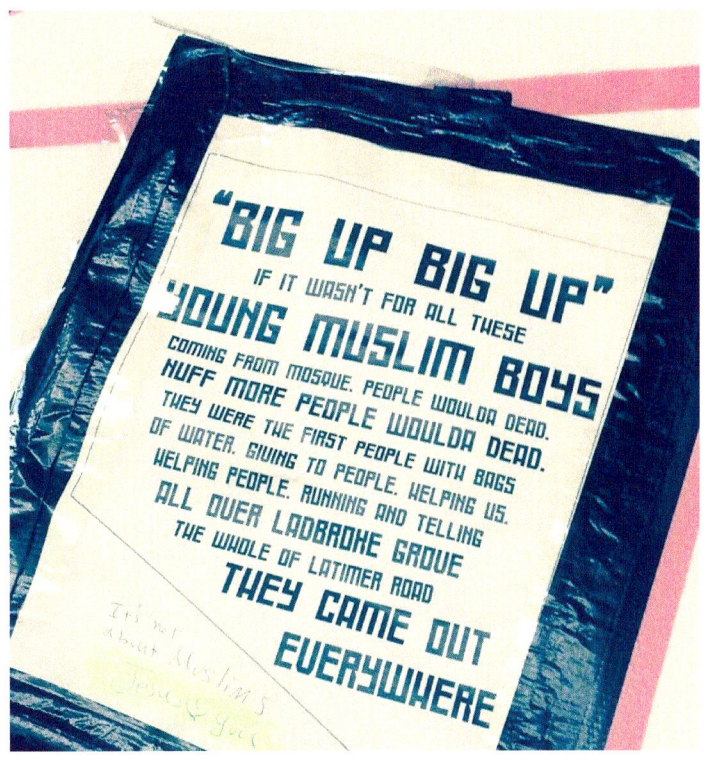

Bless, that young boys came out of the Mosques

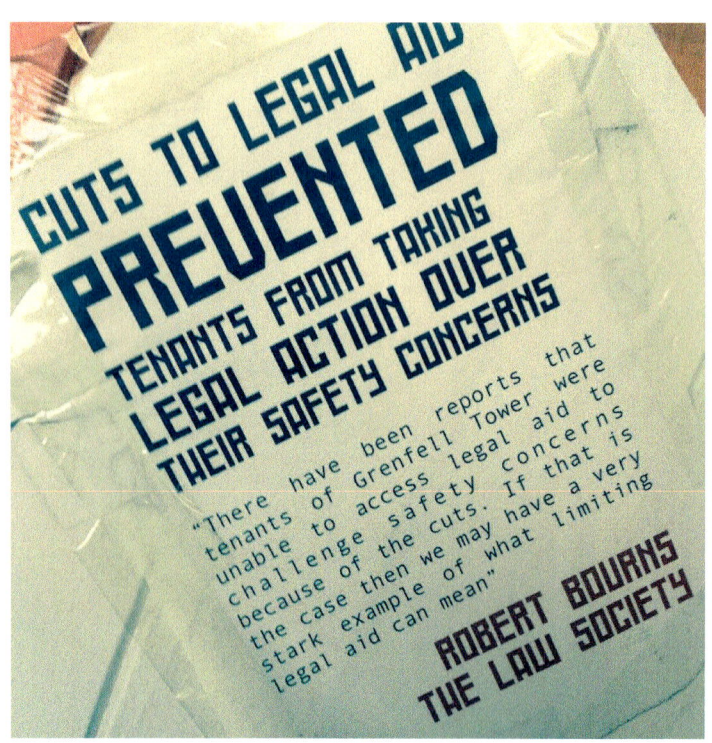

Cuts to legal aid have dire consequences

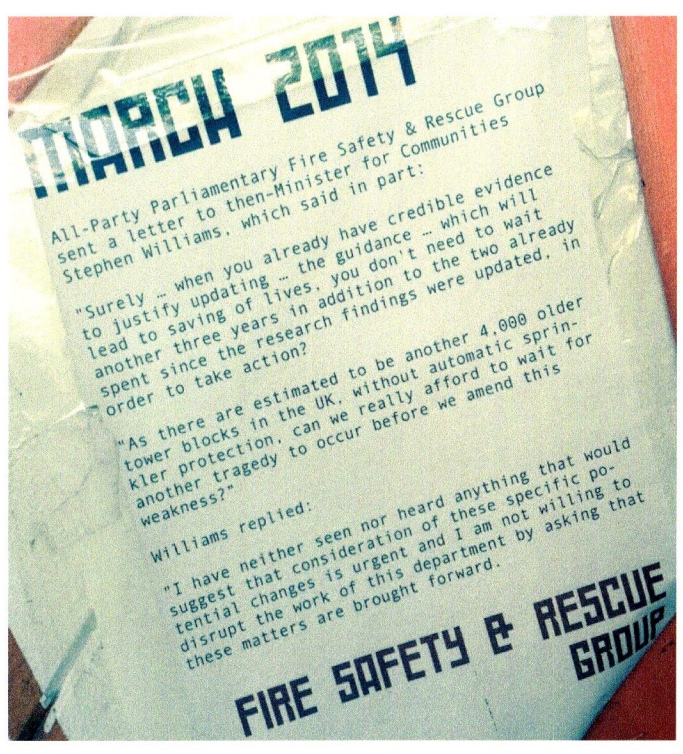

MARCH 2014

All-Party Parliamentary Fire Safety & Rescue Group sent a letter to then-Minister for Communities Stephen Williams, which said in part:

"Surely ... when you already have credible evidence to justify updating ... the guidance ... which will lead to saving of lives, you don't need to wait another three years in addition to the two already spent since the research findings were updated, in order to take action?

"As there are estimated to be another 4,000 older tower blocks in the UK, without automatic sprinkler protection, can we really afford to wait for another tragedy to occur before we amend this weakness?"

Williams replied:

"I have neither seen nor heard anything that would suggest that consideration of these specific potential changes is urgent and I am not willing to disrupt the work of this department by asking that these matters are brought forward.

FIRE SAFETY & RESCUE GROUP

Action not taken despite evidence to protect life

Justice for Grenfell

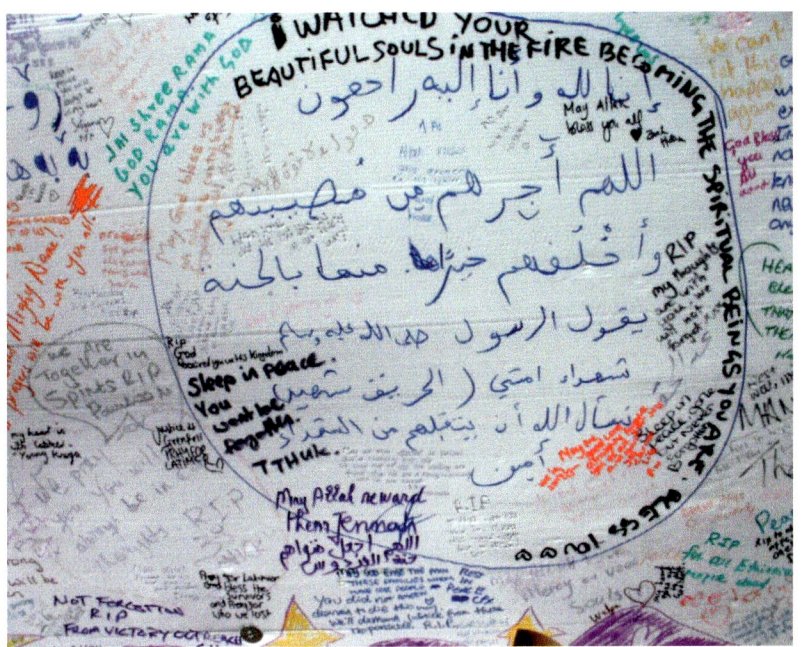

Depth of Feelings

Never alone in the Oneness

Heart of Peace

We are One in God's Love

Love within our Community

Friends and Family

Lillies of the Valley

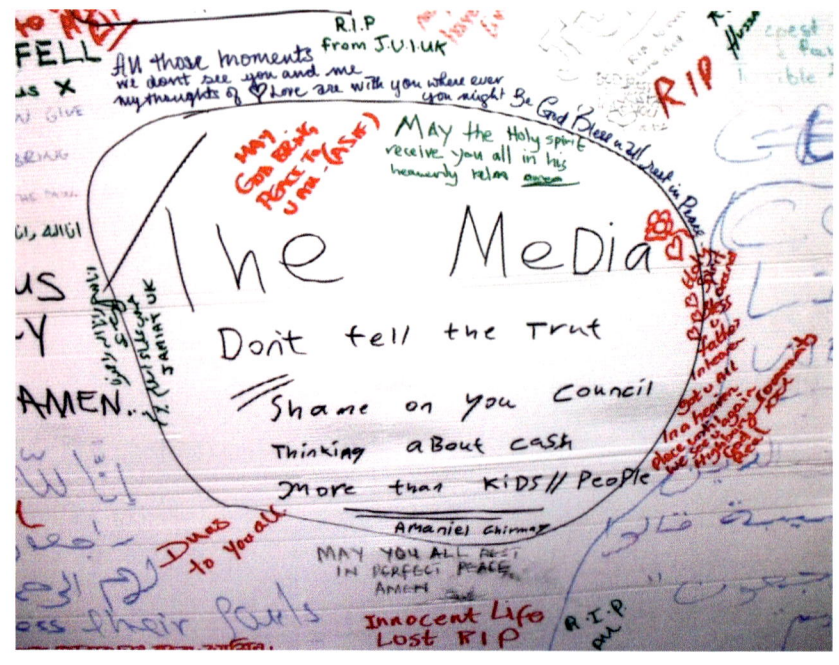

Community Not Cash

206

Loving Hearts

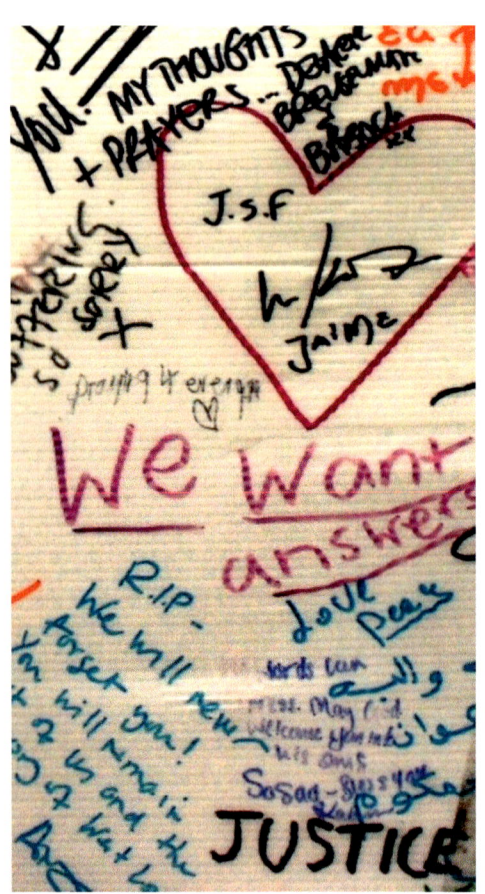

Our Prayers are with You

In the Love of God

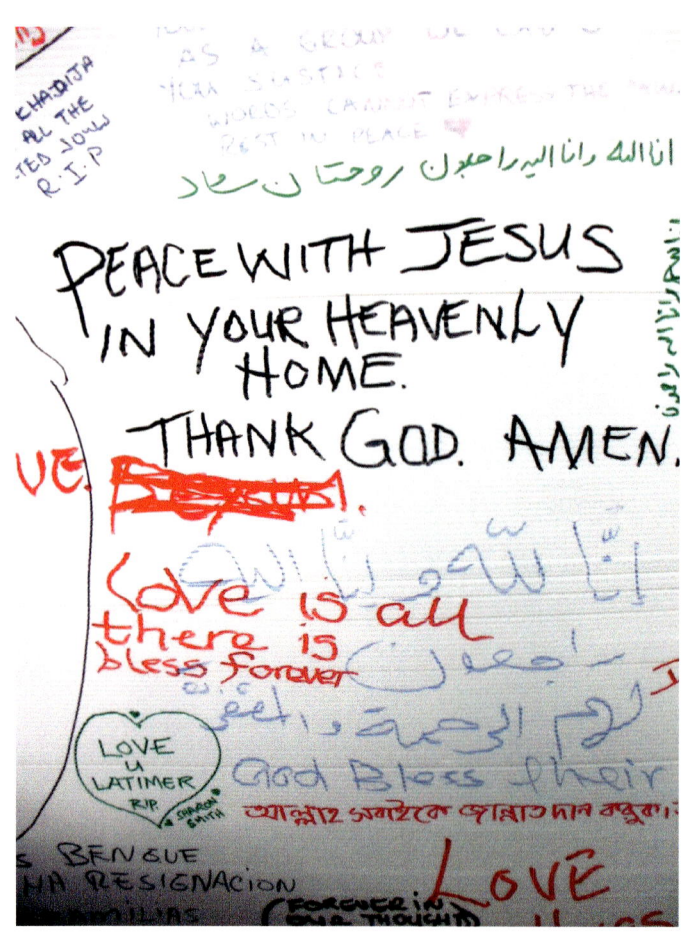

My Love Is All There Is

Here am I with all my Love

Lighting up the Light of Peace

Light Up 4 Grenfell

The Ladybird's Love for All

Ethiopian Women's Empowerment Group

Divine Mercy and Grace be with You

I Watch Over You

Mary Mother of Humanity

Poem for Grenfell

Yellow Ribbons of Hope

Blessings of Light

My heart is One with your Heart

A Prayer for Grenfell

Blessings of pure Expression

Wings of an Angel

The Truth

"And it came to me in a Dream...Humanity, because the Earth is God's Country."

Aya Samuel

REFERENCES

Introduction: Freedom and Justice

1. Court TV, Channel 179 (25 June 2021) *Outcome of Trial: Sentencing 22.5 Years*, Court TV Media LLC, Sky TV Network, Atlanta, Georgia, USA.

2. www.pewresearch.org (July 2020) *BLM 30 Million Times*, Pew Research, President Michael Dimock, Washington D.C, USA.

3. Hakim Ali, *African Migrations* (1994) Wayland Publishers Ltd., East Sussex BN3 13D.

4. Ian McAuley, *Black London Guide to Ethnic London* (1993) 2nd revised edition, Immel Publishing, London W15 4LW.

5. James Walvin, *Black Ivory* (1993) Fontana Press, Hammersmith, London W6 8JB.

6. PAC@75 (17 October 2020) *David Olusoga In Conversation*, *Pan-African Congress*, Viewing the Past and Looking to the Future, 75 Anniversary Celebrations, Manchester Metropolitan University.

7. Ottobah Cugoano, *Narrative of the Enslavement of Ottobah Cugoano* (1787). (Summary by Zachariah Hutchins (10 May 2021).

https://docsouth.unc.edu/neh/cugoano/summary.html

8. Olaudah Equiano, *The Life of Olaudah Equiano, or Gustavus Vassa, the African*, (1999) Dover Thrift Editions, Mineola, New York, USA.

9. Black History Month (2007) *Souvenir Brochure and Programme of Events,* Black History Month Advisory Group, by The African Sang, UK.

10. Black History Season (2012) *Theme for 2012: 200 Years of Revolution & Struggles in the African British Community,* Black History Month, Steering Group, Harrow, Middlesex HA1 3EX.

11. The Birth of A Nation (2016) *Inspired By A True Story,* A Nate Parker Film, Twentieth Century Fox Film Corporation, Home Entertainment LLC.

12. Harriet (2019) *"I'm Gonna Be Free Or Die",* Universal Pictures UK Ltd., England.

13. Cash Highest Price for Men, Women and even Children:

https://www.nps.gov/liho/learn/historyculture/freeport-doctrine.htlm.

14. www.history.com/www.ushistory.org

'The Great Sale of Slaves' includes a baby:
https://www.reddit.com/r/pics/comments/191wz7/1850s_slave_sale_poster_a_chilling_reminder_of/

15. The Fugitive Slave Acts allowed the law to make an arrest of what was considered to be a fugitive:

https://www.history.com/topics/black-history/fugitive-slave-acts

16. www.ncpeadia.org/slave-codes:

https://www.pvamu.edu/tiphc/exhibits/legal-path-to-african-american-freedom/virginia-slave-codes/

17. Uplands TV Ltd (19 October 2021) *A 1000 Years A Slave,* Executive Producer David Olusoga, Smithsonian Channel, Channel 5 Broadcasting Ltd., ITN Production, 200 Gray's Inn Road, London WC1X 8X2.

18. http://vbkelley.weebly.com/fugitive-slave-law-of-1850.html

19. Features a young adult male named Alfred who runs away: https://www.encyclopaediaofalabama.org/article/h-2125

20. College of Charleston, Avery Research Centre for African America History and Culture discussion and image of Bussa, 125 Bull Street, Charleston, SC 29424, http://avery.cofc.edu

21. https://www.nowgrenada.com/2021/03/this-day-in-history-3-march-1795-2/

22. Bicentenary of the Abolition of the Slave Trade Act 1807-2007, *Resistance: The Struggle for Freedom* (2007) Dept. for Communities, Crown Copyright, London SW1E 5DU.

23. https://www.history.com/news/the-amistad-slave-rebellion-175-years-ago

24. A Netflix Original *Emperor* (2020) Historical Drama, Written, Directed and Produced by Mark Amin, Played by Dayo Okeniyi. A Sobini Film Production with Hudlin Entertainment, USA.

25. The Civil War (1983) *Crusaders For Freedom, Leaders in the War Against Slavery,* Brother Against Brother*,* Edited by William C. Davis and the Editors, Timelife Books Inc., Alexandria, Virginia, USA.

26. Mary Prince *The Horrors of Slavery* (1831) in The History of Mary Prince A West Indian Slave related by Herself, Mary Prince, Published by Westley & A.H. Davis, Stationers Hall Court, London.

27. David Olusoga, *Civilizations First Contact The Cult of Progress* (2018) Profile Books Ltd., London WC1X 3HD.

28. Firpo W. Carr, *Germany's Black Holocaust 1890-1945* (2012) Published by Createspace, Independent Publishing Platform.

29.   https://www.un.org/en/observances/decade-people-african-descent, the theme is, "People of African descendant recognition, justice and development." (2015-2024)

International Decade for People of African Descent: www.un.org

30. Martin Luther King Jr., *The Autobiography of Martin Luther King, Jr.*, (1998) Edited by Claybourne Carson, The Heirs of Martin Luther King Estate; Little Brown & Company UK, Warner Books Inc. New York, USA.

31. WOW (9 March 2018) Women of the World Festival "No More" with *Patrisse Khan-Cullors Cofounder of BLM* in conversation at the Royal Festival Hall, Southbank Centre, London SE1 8XX.

32. *Government Fears Exposure of Slavery Legacy*, Mundo Obrero, Worker's World, Workers and Oppressed Peoples of the World Unite, USA. https://www.workers.org

33.   Malcolm X, *The Autobiography of Malcolm X* (1964) With the Assistance of Alex Hayley, Introduction by Gary Younge, Penguin Books, Strand, London WC1R ORL.

34. Good Morning Britain (26 August 2022) *The Cost of Living Crisis: Energy Bills Price Cap* up to £3549 in October 2022 with presenters Adil Ray and Kate Garraway, ITV Studios Ltd., 1 Television Centre, Wood Lane, London W12 7FA.

35. Channel 4 (11 November 2019) *The Unremembered*, About Forgotten African Soldiers Directed by John Deol, Presented by David Lammy, Channel 4 Television Corporation, 124-126 Horseferry Road, SW1P 2TX.

36. US Presidents who were enslavers:
https://www.history.com/news/how-many-u-s-presidents-owned-slaves

https://www.ushistory.org/presidentshouse/plans/exhibition.php

37. Ona Maria Judge interview in 1845, her story of freedom: https://www.ushistory.org/presidentshouse/slaves/oneyinterview.php

38. Sky News (15 April 2019) *Notre Dame Fire in France,* Sky News, Sky Studios, Grant Way, Isleworth, Middlesex, TW7 5QD.

39. Robin Walker, *Black History Matters* (2019) Dr. O. Nubia Consultant, Writer and Historian, Editor Julia Bird, The Watts Publishing Group, Victoria, London EC4Y 0DX.

40. Supreme Understanding (2016) *When the World Was Black Part Two: The Untold History of the World's First Civilizations, Ancient Civilizations* Proven Publishing, Second Edition, USA.

41. The Holy Bible (1958) *Genesis Chap. 2:7,* Authorised Trinitarian Bible Society, Tyndale House, London SW19 3NN.

42. BBC4 *Africa's Great Civilisations* (2017) Presented by H.L Gates Jr., BBC Studios Ltd., New Broadcasting House, Portland Place, London W1A 1AA.

43. Alex Hayley, *Roots* (1978) Picador Edition by Pan Books, Sixth Printing, Pan Books Ltd., London SW10 9PG.

44. https://oi.uchicago.edu (2021) *Minoans Early Greeks & African Presence in Britain 4,000 Years Ago*: Oriental Institute, University of Chicago, USA.

45. Joe Sandler Clark (2 September 2015) *Child Labour on Nestlé Farms,* www.theguardian.com/uk

46. Oliver Balch (12 February 2021) *Mars, Nestlé and Hershey to Face Child Slavery Lawsuit in USA,* www.theguardian.com/uk

47. Nelson Mandela, *Long Walk to Freedom* (1995) Abacus, Imprint of Little Brown Book Group, A Hatchette UK Company, London EC4Y 0DY.

48. LSE (30 March 2021) *Race And Democracy in America*, Khalil Gibran Muhammad, Professor of History, Race and Public Policy, Zoom event, 54 Lincoln's Inn Fields, London WC2A 2AE.

49. BBC *Mangrove* (2020) Small Axe, Written, Directed and Produced by Steve McQueen, Turbine Studios, Lammas Park, London W5 5JH.

50. BBC4 *Black Power A British Story of Resistance* (2021) Directed by George Amponsah, Executive Producer Steve McQueen, Narrated by Daniel Kaluuya, BBC Studios Ltd., New Broadcasting House, Portland Place, London W1A 1AA.

51. BBC Radio 2 (30 March 2021) *Surveillance Capitalism* by Professor Shoshana Zuboff in Social Psychology, Philosophy and Scholar, BBC Studios Ltd., New Broadcasting House, Portland Place, London W1A 1AA.

52. April Roach (23 March 2020) *Britons Face £5,000 Fine for Breaching Foreign Holiday Ban,* Evening Standard Ltd., Northcliffe House, London W8 5TT.

53. Fernando Corbalán, *The Golden Ratio* (2016) *The Mathematical World of Beauty*, National Geographic, Windmill Books, Vespa Design, Spain.

54. Evening Standard (28 August 2019) *Creating A Golden Triangle*, Homes & Property, Future London, Evening Standard Ltd., Northcliffe House, London W8 5TT.

55. Museum In Docklands (Spring Issue 2004) *Creating The West Indian Docks*, No.1 Warehouse, West Indian Quay, London E14 4AL.

56. Dalston Square (17 May 2024) James Baldwin Plaque Unveiling with Black History Walks and Nubian Jak Community Trust: https://www.stayhappening.com/e/james-balwin-plaque-unveiling-black-history-walks-E2ISWM8FONP

57. https://www.ourweekly.com/2009/06/19/ta-seti-worlds-oldest-civilization/ (see also archaeology.org with a ta-seti search).

58. Ashna Hurynag (5 October 2021) Black History Month, *Story of Ellen and William Craft* who risked everything to escape slavery; Sky News, Sky Studios, Grant Way, Isleworth, Middlesex, TW7 5QD.

59. Tony Warner, www.blackhistorywalks.co.uk
Black History Walks (2020) London SW1P 3JX.

60. The Voice Online Newspaper about race equity:

https://www.voice-online.co.uk/news/2021/07/14/report-shows-that-the-uk-government-approach-to-race-at-risk-of-failing-human-rights-obligations/

61. LSE Humanities Forum (14 October 2020) Nikole Hannah-Jones: *A Conversation on Racial Equity, Health, and Reframing the Legacy of Slavery*, Zoom event, London School of Economics, Houghton Street, London WC2A 2AE.

Apartheid In The East

1. BBC News (2 May 2024) US LA protestors hold ground despite dispersal order, Helena Humphrey reporting, BBC Studios Ltd., New Broadcasting House, Portland Place, London W1A 1AA.

2. Cameron Henderson (14 May 2024) Pro-Palestine protestors take over LSE building, The Telegraph online:

https://www.telegraph.co.uk/news/2024/05/14/palestine-protesters-lse-university-building-campus-tents/

3. News Hour (6 April/16 April 2024) Gaza Genocide: Live Feed with Tom McRae presenter *UN Human Rights to hold Israel accountable for War Crimes*, Al Jazeera Media Network, PO Box 23137, Doha Qatar.

4. News Live (11 March 2024) Gaza Genocide: *Risk of Mass Starvation*, McRae presenter, Cyprus to ship in Supplies Today, Al Jazeera Media Network, PO Box 23137, Doha Qatar.

5. News Live (13 February 2024) Gaza Genocide: No Where Is Safe *Rafah Facing Ground Assault*, LIVE from Doha, Al Jazeera Media Network, PO Box 23137, Doha Qatar.

6. News Live (11 January 2024) Headline News: *South Africa Brings Case of Genocide* to International Court of Justice, LIVE from The Hague, Osman Bin Javaid reporting, Al Jazeera Media Network, PO Box 23137, Doha Qatar.

7. News Hour (22 December 2023) *Children's Protest in Westminster*, London, Sonia Gallego reporting, Al Jazeera Media Network, PO Box 23137, Doha Qatar.

8. The Stream (5 December 2023) Assets:*$124 Billion Since WWII* an Investment in Genocide; Israel Trains US Policing Claudia de La Cruz, New York Party for Socialism and Liberation, Al Jazeera Media Network, PO Box 23137, Doha Qatar.

9. News Hour (7 December 2023) Hostages Confirm: *Israeli Helicopters Airstrike at Festival*, Imran Khan reporting from Tel. Aviv, Israel, Al Jazeera Media Network, PO Box 23137, Doha Qatar.

10. News Hour (19 November 2023) Haaretz Investigations: *Israeli Army Helicopters Airstrikes at Festival*, according to the

Jewish Newspaper, LIVE Headline News, Al Jazeera Media Network, PO Box 23137, Doha Qatar.

11. News Hour (4 November 2023) War Crimes: *Israel in Violation of International Law*, Nicolas Haque in Darkar, UNRWA LIVE in Jordan; Mass Protest in Several Countries, Al Jazeera Media Network, PO Box 23137, Doha Qatar.

12. A Summary of the UN Convention on the Rights of the Child, Unicef, United Kingdom.

UNCRC_summary-1_1.pdf and www.unicef.org.uk

13. News Hour (11 November 2023) Gaza Genocide: *Calls for Summit to Investigate Israeli War Crimes*, comments of Senior Political Analysis Marwan Bishara, Al Jazeera Media Network, PO Box 23137, Doha Qatar.

14. News Hour (14 November 2023) Gaza Genocide: *Mass Protest in Manila Philippines*; Palestinian Rights Groups File A Genocide Lawsuit in the USA, Al Jazeera Media Network, PO Box 23137, Doha.

15. News Hour (17 November 2023) Gaza Genocide: *Mass Protest for a Ceasefire* in Jordon, Lebanon, Yemen, South Korea, Al Jazeera Media Network, PO Box 23137, Doha Qatar.

16. News Hour (11 November 2023) Gaza Genocide: *Mass Protest For a Ceasefire*, London Protest, over 700,000 Protestors, protest in South Africa, Indonesia, Delaware USA, Al Jazeera Media Network, PO Box 23137, Doha Qatar.

17. News Live/News Hour (10, 11, 12 & 15 November 2023) Gaza Genocide: *Al Shifa Hospital Suffers More Shelling, Airstrikes, Gunfire and Raids*, Hani Mahmoud reports, Transgression of International Law by Israel; reports too by Maleen Saeed:

Inside Al Shifa by Dr Muhammed Abu Salmiya, Director of Al Shifa Hospital and Mustafa Sarsour reporting, Al Jazeera Media Network, PO Box 23137, Doha Qatar.

18. Good Morning Britain (13 November 2023) War on Gaza: *LIVE Interview with Dr. Mena EL-Farra*, Founder of the AL Awda Children's Hospital and Basma Ghalayini, ITV Studios Ltd., 1 Television Centre, Wood Lane, London W12 7FA.

19. BBC Breakfast (5 November 2023) LIVE from Goring-On-Thames, Story of Dr Abdelkader Hammond, BBC Studios Ltd., New Broadcasting House, Portland Place, London W1A 1AA.

20. News Live (30 November 2023) Gaza Genocide: *Indiscriminate Shooting* of 8-year-old Adam Ghoul and his friend 15-year-old Basel Suleiman shot while playing, Al Jazeera Media Network, PO Box 23137, Doha Qatar.

21. News Hour (16 November 2023) Headline News: *Shortages of Food, Water and Fuel Used As Weapon*, Philippe Lazzarini, Commissioner-General, UNRWA, LIVE UN Geneva, Al Jazeera Media Network, PO Box 23137, Doha Qatar.

22. Sky News Today (17 October 2023) Breaking News: *Hospitals Will Run Out of Fuel*, LIVE with Jayne Secker presenter, Doctors Without Borders Humanitarian Affairs Manager, Friederike Van Dongen, Al Jazeera Media Network, PO Box 23137, Doha Qatar.

Stopped Searched Shot or Killed

1. Angelique Chrisafis (27 June 2023) https://www.theguardian.com/world/2023/jun/27/police-officer-investigated-boy-shot-dead-paris-nanterre

2. ITV Evening News (28 January 2023) *Video Released by Police Showing Brutality Toward Tyre Nichols*, Robert Moore

reporting from Memphis, Tennessee; ITV Studios Ltd., 1 Television Centre, Wood Lane, London W12 7FA.

3. BBC News (27 January 2023) *Tyre's Mother Calls for Calm and Shows Mercy* to the Officers, BBC Studios Ltd., New Broadcasting House, Portland Place, London W1A 1AA.

4. https://twitter.com/blklivesmatter (27 January 2023) *Tyre A Gifted Skateboarder and Photographer*, Twitter Inc., San Francisco, California, USA.

5. https://www.theguardian.com/us-news/2021/sep/22/us-police-reform-bill-congress-bipartisan-talks

6. https://twitter.com/UFFCampaign (27 January 2023) *UN Findings Britain is Institutional, Structural and Systemically Racist*, Twitter Inc., San Francisco, California, USA.

7. Sky News (17 December 2022) *The Killing of Chris Kaba* an investigation into his death and delays in seeking justice, Shingi Mararike reporting; Sky News, Sky Studios, Grant Way, Isleworth, Middlesex, TW7 5QD.

8. https://www.theguardian.com/uk-news/2022/sep/17/protest-uk-met-police-killing-black-chris-kaba

https://www.theguardian.com/uk-news/2022/sep/25/chris-kabas-family-back-call-for-un-to-examine-police-shooting

9. Good Morning Britain (16 August 2022) *Ricardo Racially Profiled and Stopped by Police*, ITV Studios Ltd., 1 Television Centre, Wood Lane, London W12 7FA.

10. BBC3 *You Match The Description: Stop & Search* (2020) presented by Aaron Roach-Bridgeman, Filmed, Edited and

Directed by Cebo Luthuli; BBC Studios Ltd., New Broadcasting House, Portland Place, London W1A 1AA.

11. BBC3 *Fighting The Power* (2020) Filmed, Produced and Directed by Eddie Hutton-Mils; BBC Studios Ltd., New Broadcasting House, Portland Place, London W1A 1AA.

12. Good Morning Britain (5 May 2022) *Mistrust In The Police Rises*, Presented by Adil Ray and Kate Garraway, ITV Studios Ltd., 1 Television Centre, Wood Lane, London W12 7FA.

13. Good Morning Britain (8 August 2022) *Strip Searches Traumatise Children* presented by Adil Ray and Charlotte Hawkins, an interview with Dame Rachel de Souza, ITV Studios Ltd., 1 Television Centre, Wood Lane, London W12 7FA.

14. Mauricio Peňo/Alex Hernandez (April 2 2021) *The Shooting of 13-Year-Old Adam Toledo*:

www.blockclubchicago.org

https://news.sky.com (16 April 2021) *Protest for Adam Toledo*, Sky News, USA.

15. Brendan O'Brien (16 April 2021) *The Shooting of Adam Toledo*: "Stop Racist Police Terror!"

https://www.reuters.com/journalists/brendan-obrien

16. "Stop Killing Our Children 48 hours Cover Up!" (16 April 2021).

www.sky.news.com

17. Mitch Smith (13 April 2022) *The Shooting of Patrick Lyoya*:

https://www.nytimes.com/2022/13/us/grand-rapids-policeshooting-michigan-patrick-lyoya.html

18. CNN Early Start (13 April 2021) *The Shooting of Daunte Wright*, Josh Campbell reporting from Minnesota, with presenters Laura Jarrett and Christine Romans, Cable News Network, Atlanta, Georgia, USA.

19. Good Morning Britain (13 April 2021) *The Shooting of Daunte Wright*, with Adil Ray, Kate Garraway and Rev. Mark Thompson by LIVE video link and Noel Phillips reporting from Minnesota, USA, ITV Studios Ltd., 1 Television Centre, Wood Lane, London W12 7FA.

20. BBC News (22 April 2021) *Larry Madowo Reporting LIVE from Minneapolis*, Shiloh Temple International Ministries with presenters Katty Kay and Christian Fraser, New Broadcasting House, Portland Place, London W1A 1AA.

21. www.twitter.com/abc4news (23 August 2020) *The Shooting of Jacob Blake*, Twitter Inc., San Francisco, California, USA.

22. https://twitter.com/home (24 August 2020) *My Tweet about Jacob Blake who was shot 7 times in his back by brutal police officers,* Twitter Inc., San Francisco, California, USA.

23. BBC News London (26 August 2020) *Father's Reaction to the Shooting of Jacob Blake*, BBC Studios Ltd., New Broadcasting House, Portland Place, London W1A 1AA.

24. A Netflix Original *Two Distant Strangers* (2021) Written by Jo Vaughn Virginia, Directed by Travon Free and Martin Desmond Roe, Sag-Aftra Endeavor Content, USA.

25. ITN Channel 4 News (11 August 2023) *Jamar Powell Wrongfully Stopped and Searched*, reported by Ria Chatterjee, Channel 4 News, Television Corporation, 124-126 Horseferry Road, London SW1P 2TX.

BLM Protest Brutality

1. CNN Blitzer (30 May 2020) *Mass Protest After the Killing of George Floyd*, Wisconsin, Minnesota, Cable News Network, Atlanta, Georgia, USA.

2. CNN Network (8 June 2020) *Martin Luther King III and Derrick Johnson,* CEO of NAACP, Cable News Network, Atlanta, Georgia, USA.

3. BBC News (15 March 2021) *Grammy Awards, CBS/recording Academy,* Los Angeles, USA; BBC Studios Ltd., New Broadcasting House, Portland Place, London W1A 1AA.

4. CNN Network (9 June 2020) *"Equal Justice Under The Law",* Al Sharpton's Eulogy, for George Floyd, The Fountain of Praise Church, Houston, Texas.

5. Good Morning Britain (21 April 2021) *All Three Counts of the Guilty Verdict, Justice for George Floyd*, LIVE video link with aunt Angela Harrelson and cousin Paris Stevens, with presenter Adil Ray, ITV Studios Ltd., 1 Television Centre, Wood Lane, London W12 7FA.

6. Court TV, Channel 179 (29 March 2021) *The Trial Begins: Justice for George Floyd*, White Male Officer had his knee on George's neck for over 9 minutes, Plus the Verdict, Court TV Media LLC, Sky TV Network, Atlanta, Georgia USA.

7. Isabel Keane (2022) https://metro.co.uk/2022/02/24/three-ex-cops-convicted-of-rights-violations-in-george-floyd-killing-16170169/

8. CNN Early Start (30 March 2021) *Donald Williams, Witness Testimony in the case of George Floyd*, Minnesota, Cable News Network, Atlanta, Georgia, USA.

9. Sky News (5 April 2021) *Doctor B.W. Lengenfeld, Witness Testimony*, Televised Proceedings in the Trial Justice For George Floyd, Minnesota, Sarah Lockwood reporting in the USA; Sky News, Sky Studios, Grant Way, Isleworth, Middlesex, TW7 5QD.

10. Jeremy Vine (6 April 2021) *Chief Arradondo Witness Testimony*, Channel 5 Broadcasting Ltd., Camden, London; Viacom CBS Network, Televised Proceedings from Minnesota, USA.

11. Baltimore Rising (2017) *The Death of Freddie Grey*, Directed by Sonja Sohn, HBO Films, USA.

12. Sky News (7 June 2020) *Protest: A Rising Up Against the Systems that Built the Western World,* Anthony Cook, Professor of Law, George Town University, D.C, USA; Sky News, Sky Studios, Grant Way, Isleworth, Middlesex, TW7 5QD.

Stand Up To Racism

1. Reuters (31 May 2024) Britain's opposition Labour Party said that *Diane Abbott, Britain's first Black woman lawmaker,* would be able to run in the July 4 election:

https://www.reuter.com/world/uk/uk-actors-writer-call-out-systemic-racism-over-abbott-treatment-20234-05-31/

2. 5 News @ 5 (21 February 2023) *Medical Student Korrine Sky Experience exiting Ukraine,* presenter Claudia-Liza Vanderpuije, Chan 5 LIVE, Broadcasting Ltd., ITN Production, 200 Gray's Inn Road, London WC1X 8X2.

3. https://buffalonews.com/news/local/crime-and-courts/buffalos-worst-mass-shooting-takes-10-lives-leaves-3-wounded-attack-called-a-racially-motivated/article_6e8132fa-d3b7-11ec-a714-2b3fbeaf848c.html

4. CNN Newsroom (6 March 2022) *African Students Face Racial Discrimination At The Border*, LIVE with Sarah Newton Presented by Kim Brunhuber, Cable News Network, Atlanta, Georgia, USA.

5. Lester Holloway (27 February 2022) *African students trapped in Ukraine*:

https://www.voice-online.co.uk/news/world-news/2022/02/27/hundreds-of-africans-trapped-in-ukraine-warzone/#.YhuFJ8o78OM.twitter

6. BBC News (1 March 2022) Marcus Ryder representing *Centre for Diversity in Media and AMEJA* (Arab & Middle Eastern Journalist Association) BBC Studios Ltd., New Broadcasting House, Portland Place, London W1A 1AA.

7. https://www.savethechildren.net/news/number-children-living-deadliest-war-zones-rises-nearly-20-highest-over-decade-%E2%80%93-save-children

United Nations High Commission for Refugees (2022)

https://www.unhcr.org/uk/figures-at-a-glance.html

8. WNO (Windrush National Organisation)

Retweet to WHO about Lewin William, 74 with cancer to be deported back to Jamaica, Twitter Inc., San Francisco, California,

USA. https://twitter.com/home

9. Jessica Muray/V.Dodd (2 June 2021) *14-Year-old Dea-John Reid was killed by a racist*: www.theguardian.com/uk

10. https://twitter.com/home (25 May 2021) *Retweet about the shooting of Sasha Johnson,* BLM Activist, Twitter Inc., San Francisco, California, USA.

11. Anthony France,(1March2022) https://www.standard.co.uk/news/crime/sasha-johnson-shot-mother-emotional-appeal-london-peckham-blm-b985155.html

12. Professor Kehinde Andrews (14 October 2020) In Conversation, *Do Black Lives Matter?* Black Studies, Zoom event, University of Birmingham.

13. PAC@75 (18 October 2020) *Lemn Sissay In Conversation, Pan-African Congress,* Viewing the Past and Looking to the Future, 75 Anniversary, Manchester Metropolitan University.

14. ITV Evening News (3 January 2023) *The Legendary Pelé Is Laid to Rest With A Military Ceremony,* Steve Scott reporting from Santos, Brazil, ITV Studios Ltd., 1 Television Centre, Wood Lane, London W12 7FA.

15. Good Morning Britain (13 July 2021) *Silencing Racist Abuse Online with Psychologist John Amaechi,* ITV Studios Ltd., 1 Television Centre, Wood Lane, London W12 7FA.

16. Good Morning Britain (8 & 9 March 2021) *Harry & Meghan Interview with Oprah Winfrey,* Exclusive CBS, This Morning, ITV Studios Ltd., 1 Television Centre, Wood Lane, London W12 7FA.

17. ITV News London (22 February 2023) *Shola Mos-Shogbaminu Receives Death Threats,* presenter Lucrezia Millarini, ITV Studios Ltd., 1 Television Centre, Wood Lane, London W12 7FA.

18. The Stephen Lawrence Inquiry (15 February 1999) *Chap. 6: Racism, 6.5. The Inquiry Into the Death of Stephen Lawrence* By

Sir William Macpherson of Cluny, Published by the Stationary Office Ltd., P.O Box 276, London SW8 5DT.

19. ITV News (22 April 2021) *The Legacy of Steven Lawrence*, Steven Lawrence Day, ITV Studios Ltd., 1 Television Centre, Wood Lane, London W12 7FA.

20. Vic Motune (31 March 2022) *Shopping While Black* https://www.voice-online.co.uk/news/features-news/2022/03/31/shopping-while-black/

21. Sinai Fleary (24 February 2022) *Black People Facing Housing Discrimination* With Campaigner Twajo Tweneboa:

https://www.voice-online.co.uk/news/uk-news/2022/02/24/black-tenants-living-in-inhumane-social-housing-says-leading-campaigner/

22. Stand Up To Racism (22 May 2021)*, Take The Knee For George Floyd*, Online protest, SUTR, PO Box, 72710, London. www.standuptoracism.org.uk

Covid Uncovered

1. Worldometers (8 June 2024) update on number of fatalities due to coronavirus:

https://www.worldometers.info/coronavirus/country/uk/
https://www.worldometers.info/coronavirus/country/usa/

2. Jeremy Vine (13 May 2021) *Lobby Akinnola Representing Covid Bereaved Families for Justice*, Channel 5 Broadcasting Ltd., ITN Production, 200 Gray's Inn Road, London WC1X 8X2.

3. Good Morning Britain (5 April 2021) *Dr Amir Khan's Reaction to Institutional Racism*, ITV Studios Ltd., 1 Television Centre, Wood Lane, London W12 7FA.

4. Sky News (7 May 2020) *Office of National Statistics Chart*, Sky News, Sky Studios, Grant Way, Isleworth, Middlesex, TW7 5QD.

5. BBC News (16 April 2020) *Research Data Black and Asian Disproportionate Covid Treatment*, Rhianna Croxford Health Correspondent, ICU (Intensive Care Units) BBC Studios Ltd., New Broadcasting House, Portland Place, London W1A 1AA.

6. Haroon Saddique (10 April 2020) *UK Government Urged to Investigate Coronavirus Deaths*:

https://www.theguardian.com/society/2020/apr/10uk-coronvirus-deaths-bame-doctors-bma

7. Good Morning Britain (22 February 2021) *Deemed Unlawful To Not Have PPE* for Medical and Social Care Staff, ITV Studios Ltd., 1 Television Centre, Wood Lane, London W12 7FA.

Reparations March

1. Grant Gallacher (28 March 2024) *Should Reparations Be Paid to Slave Descendants?* UK Survey Shows Growing Support

https://edge.media/slavery-reparations

2. Ben Lindsay (29 October 2019) *We Need to Talk About Race: Black Experience*, St. Paul's Cathedral, London EC14M 8AD.

3. Leah Mahon (August 2023) *£18 Trillion What Britain Owes in Reparations,* The Voice Newspaper, Unit 1, Bricklayers Arms, Mandela Way, London SE1 5SR.

4. Reporter (2013) *Britain's Debt to Slavery*, Anti-Slavery Magazine, Issue Spring 2013, Anti-Slavery International, Thomas Clarkson House, The Stableyard, Broomgrove Road, London SW9 9TL.

5. Sky News (19 March 2021) *Financial Reparations*, Sarah Lockwood reporting from Illinois, Evanston, Chicago, USA; Sky News, Sky Studios, Grant Way, Isleworth, Middlesex TW7 5QD.

United Family & Friends Campaign

1. www.uffc.org.uk (1998) *United Friends And Family Campaign* (UFFC) Institute of Race Relations, Kings Cross Road, London WC1X.

2. www.inquest.org

Truth, Justice, Accountability, Institute of Race Relations, Kings Cross Road, London WC1X.

3. Tippa Naphtali

https://4wardeveruk.org/2018/04/deaths-in-custody-point-to-structural-racism-in-britain-says-un-panel/

Windrush Betrayal

1. Helen William (18 June 2019) *Windrush Scandal dates from 1950s hostile MPs'* Metro, Northcliffe House, London W8 5TT.

2. Flora Thompson (21 May 2021) *Windrush Victims Facing Long Waits for Compensation*, Evening Standard Ltd., Northcliffe House, London W8 5TT.

3. Amelia Gentlemen (12 May 2021) *Anthony Brown: the man who resisted deportation – Then fought tirelessly for Windrush survivors*. www.theguardian.com/uk

4. Retweet (13 November 2019) to *Nadine White on the Experience of Hubert Howard,* Twitter Inc., San Francisco, California, USA. https://twitter.com/home

5. Equality and Human Rights Commission, UK (25 November 2020) *Section 149 of the Equality Act* 2010:

https://www.equalityhumanrights.com/en/inquiries-and-investigations/assessment-hostile-environment-policies

Remembering Grenfell

1. ITV News (15 February 2021) *From Grenfell Inquiry: It was known that the Cladding was Flammable*, presented and reported by Rags Martel, ITV Studios Ltd., 1 Television Centre, Wood Lane, London W12 7FA.

Black Lives Matter

1. Jermaine Houghton (29 July 2013) *Protesters March in Honour of Trayvon Martin*:
http://www.voice-online.co.uk/article/london-protesters-march-trayvon-martin

2. Mark Townsend (3 September 2017) *Four Black Men Die. Did police action play a part?*

https://www.theguardian.com/uk-news/2017/sep/03/four-black-men-die-police-restraint-no-officers-suspended-bryant-cumberbatch-charles-da-costa

https://www.theguardian.com/uk-news/2017/jul/24/angry-protesters-challenge-police-over-death-of-rashan-charles

https://www.theguardian.com/us-news/2016/jul/09/black-lives-matter-rallies-hundreds-in-second-uk-day-of-protest

3. https://twitter.com/home (26 July 2017) *My Tweet About Justice & Accountability for the Lives of Black Men,* Twitter Inc., San Francisco, California, USA.

4. https://edition.cnn.com/2016/07/07/us/shootings-alton-sterling-philando-castile/index.html

Grenfell Remembrance Walls

1. Good Morning Britain (14 June 2017) *Breaking News: Fatalities Confirmed in Tower Block,* Major Fire Rips Through Tower Block in West London; ITV Studios Ltd., 1 Television Centre, Wood Lane, London W12 7FA.

Aya Samuel has a BA in Sociology & Media and is an activist for social justice. She lives in London and enjoys true life drama, films, adventure, comedy, singing, listening to music and events. She would love to experience the great wonders of the world and many amazing places and people. She enjoys relaxing in scenic places or with an urban beat. She is also planning to support the planting of new trees in the giving to the Earth Mother.